The Fat Lady Dances:
MARGARET ATWOOD'S

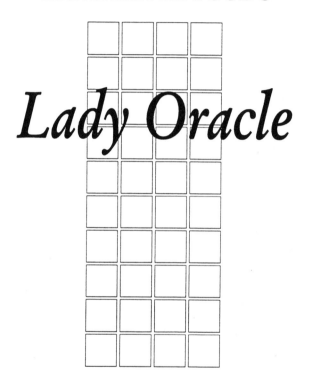

Lady Oracle

Margery Fee

ECW PRESS

Learning Resources
Centre
Copyright © ECW PRESS, 1993

CANADIAN CATALOGUING IN PUBLICATION DATA

Fee, Margery, 1948–
The fat lady dances : Margaret Atwood's Lady oracle

(Canadian fiction studies ; 15)
Includes bibliographical references and index.
ISBN 1–55022–136–1
1. Atwood, Margaret, 1939– . Lady oracle.
I. Title. II. Series.

PS8501.T86L334 1993   C813'.54   C91-095017-2
PR9199.3.A78L334 1993

This book has been published with the assistance of the
Ministry of Culture and Communications of the Province
of Ontario, through funds provided by the Ontario
Publishing Centre, and with the assistance of grants from
The Canada Council, the Ontario Arts Council, and the
Government of Canada through the Department of
Communications, and the Canadian Studies and Special Projects
Directorate of the Department of the Secretary of State of Canada.

The cover features a reproduction of the dust-wrapper from the
first edition of Lady Oracle, courtesy of McClelland and Stewart.
Frontispiece photograph by Graeme Gibson.
Design and imaging by ECW Type & Art, Oakville, Ontario.
Printed and bound by Hignell Printing, Winnipeg, Manitoba.

Distributed by General Publishing Co. Limited
30 Lesmill Road, Don Mills, Ontario M3B 2T6

Published by ECW PRESS,
1980 Queen Street East,
Toronto, Ontario M4L 1J2

Table of Contents

☐ A Note on the Author ☐

Margery Fee was born in London, Ontario, and grew up in the Toronto suburb of Etobicoke, where she was a Brownie. She earned all her degrees in Toronto: her B.A. in English and French at Glendon College, her M.A. at York University, and her Ph.D. at the University of Toronto. She also has a Diploma in Applied Linguistics from the University of Victoria. After working as a teaching fellow at University College, the University of Toronto, she taught at the University of Saskatchewan, the University of Victoria, and Queen's University, where she is currently a member of the Department of English and the Director of the Strathy Language Unit. The unit undertakes research into Canadian English and English usage. Her work on Canadian literature includes articles on Jeannette Armstrong, Ernest Buckler, Beatrice Culleton, Marian Engel, Howard O'Hagan, Lorne Pierce, and various aspects of literary nationalism. She has also published work on the New Zealand writer Keri Hulme and on Canadian English.

NOTE ON EDITIONS AND REFERENCES

Lady Oracle was first published in Canada by Seal–McClelland and Stewart in 1976. The Seal–McClelland and Stewart–Bantam paperback edition was published in 1977, and all page references in this work are to this 1977 edition. *Lady Oracle* was also published in New York by Simon and Schuster in 1976, and in London by André Deutsch in 1977.

The Fat Lady Dances:
Margaret Atwood's
Lady Oracle

Chronology

1939   Margaret Atwood born 18 November in Ottawa, the second of three children. Her elder brother Harold was born in 1937. Her father is Carl Edmund Atwood, a forest entomologist, specializing in bees, the spruce budworm, and forest tent caterpillars. Her mother, Margaret Dorothy (Killam), is a graduate in home economics from the University of Toronto.

1939–45   Family lives in Ottawa in the winters and spends the rest of the year in northern Quebec and Ontario, where father conducts research.

1945–46   Family moves briefly to Sault Ste. Marie.

1946   Family settles in Toronto, where father teaches at University of Toronto.

1951   Younger sister, Ruth, is born.

1952–57   Studies at Leaside High School, Toronto; contributes prose and verse to school literary magazine.

1958   Works at Camp White Pine, Haliburton, in charge of the nature hut, where she meets Charles Pachter, in charge of arts and crafts.

1957–61   Honours English student at Victoria College, University of Toronto; studies with Northrop Frye, Jay Macpherson, Kathleen Coburn, Millar MacLure; submits literary work to college magazines, cowrites articles with Dennis Lee.

1961   *Double Persephone* (poetry) wins E.J. Pratt Medal. Wins Woodrow Wilson Fellowship on graduation.

1961–62   Graduate studies in English at Radcliffe College, Harvard

University; studies Victorian literature under Jerome H. Buckley. Gains her M.A.

1962–63   Doctoral studies, Harvard University.

1963–64   Works for a market research company in Toronto; writes unpublished novel *Up in the Air So Blue*.

1964–65   Teaches English at the University of British Columbia.

1965–67   Continues doctoral studies at Harvard; completes all the requirements except for the dissertation, "The English Metaphysical Romance," focusing on novelist H. Rider Haggard.

1966   *The Circle Game* (poetry).

1967   Wins Governor-General's Award for *The Circle Game*. Marries James Polk, fellow graduate student and American novelist.

1967–68   Teaches English at Sir George Williams University (now part of Concordia University) in Montreal.

1968   *The Animals in That Country* (poetry); moves to Edmonton.

1969   *The Edible Woman* (novel).

1969–70   Teaches creative writing at the University of Alberta.

1970   *Procedures for Underground* (poetry); *The Journals of Susanna Moodie* (poetry).

1970–71   Travels in England, France, and Italy.

1971   *Power Politics* (poetry); begins to serve as editor and member of the board of House of Anansi Press (continues until 1973).

1971–72   Teaches Canadian literature at York University, Toronto.

1972   *Surfacing* (novel); *Survival: A Thematic Guide to Canadian Literature* (literary criticism).

1972–73   Writer in residence at the University of Toronto.

1973   Divorces James Polk; moves to Alliston, Ontario, with Graeme Gibson, Canadian writer (*Five Legs* [1969]; *Communion* [1971]; *Perpetual Motion* [1982]). Awarded by Trent University the first of her many honorary degrees.

1974   *You Are Happy* (poetry).

1973–75	Member of the Board of Directors of the Canadian Civil Liberties Association.
1975	Begins to contribute a comic strip called *Kanadian Kultchur Komix* featuring "Survivalwoman" to the left-wing nationalist *This Magazine*, under the name Bart Gerrard.
1976	*Lady Oracle* (novel; winner of the City of Toronto Book Award [1977] and the Canadian Booksellers Association Award [1977]); *Selected Poems*; daughter Jess (Eleanor Jess Atwood Gibson) is born.
1977	*Dancing Girls* (short stories; which receives St. Lawrence Award for Fiction and the Periodical Distributors of Canada Award for Short Fiction); *Days of the Rebels, 1815–1840* (history).
1978	Visits Australia for Writers' Week; *Two-Headed Poems*; *Up in the Tree* (children's book); becomes a contributing editor to *This Magazine*.
1978–79	Lives in Scotland while Gibson teaches at the University of Edinburgh.
1979	*Life Before Man* (novel).
1980	Family moves to Toronto; *Anna's Pet* (children's story; with Joyce Barkhouse; adapted for stage in 1986).
1980–81	Vice-chair of Writers' Union of Canada.
1981	*True Stories* (poetry); *Bodily Harm* (novel).
1982	*Second Words: Selected Critical Prose*. Edits *The New Oxford Book of Canadian Verse in English*.
1982–83	President of Writers' Union of Canada.
1983	*Murder in the Dark: Short Fictions and Prose Poems*; *Bluebeard's Egg* (short stories).
1983–84	Travels and works in England and Germany.
1984	*Interlunar* (poetry).
1984–85	President of P.E.N. International's Anglo-Canadian branch; P.E.N. promotes friendship among writers, supports freedom of expression, and pressures for the release of writers who are political prisoners.
1985	*The Handmaid's Tale* (novel; winner, in 1986, of both the Governor-General's Award and the Los Angeles *Times*

Award); MFA Chair, Creative Writing, University of Alabama, Tuscaloosa.

1986   Coeditor with Robert Weaver of *The Oxford Book of Canadian Short Stories in English*. Berg Chair, Creative Writing, New York University. *Selected Poems II: Poems Selected and New, 1976–1986*; *The Festival of Missed Crass* (children's musical); writer in residence, Macquarie University, Sydney, Australia.

1988   *Cat's Eye* (novel), wins City of Toronto Book Award.

1991   *Wilderness Tips* (short stories), wins Trillium Award.

1992   *Good Bones* (short fictions and prose poems).

The Importance of the Work

After *Surfacing* (1972), Atwood's gloomy and gripping second novel, *Lady Oracle* (1976), her third, may seem at first glance simply a piece of comic relief. *Surfacing* is narrated by a severely depressed woman who struggles to come to terms with her abortion and the deaths of her parents. The story is set in a wilderness threatened by pollution in a Canada that is rapidly selling out to the highest bidder. *Lady Oracle* seems to have more in common with Atwood's comic first novel, *The Edible Woman* (1969), where Marian McAlpin, like Joan Foster, somewhat ineptly frees herself from an unsatisfactory relationship with the ambiguous assistance of some eccentric friends.

The reader can understand both these heroines' problems fairly well, and certainly sees long before either Marian or Joan does that they will have to disentangle themselves from the men who are central to their lives. Unfortunately, the distance between what the reader understands and the understanding of these characters is so great that it is tempting to dismiss them as airheads. Instead of identifying with their difficulties in finding interesting occupations and interested partners, the reader may well feel that any idiot could manage better than these two, who ricochet from crisis to crisis on some kind of intuition-driven automatic pilot. If this is our only reaction, these novels may well delight us without teaching us, and good novels are supposed to do both.

But these overtly comic novels do have a serious side. Atwood seems to be examining how women can be trapped by upbringing, education, and social expectations in relationships where they give up thinking about their own needs completely. (Perhaps airheads are made rather than born?) All that saves Marian and Joan in the end (if they are saved) is a kind of emotional or physiological reflex. (Marian knows she's in trouble when she can no longer eat, Joan, when she has hallucinations of her mother.) The importance of both these novels comes not just from their comic surface, then, but also from their rather darker underside. This dark side is clearly represented in *Lady Oracle* by Joan's occupation as a writer of Gothic romances filled with terrified young women. By making Joan a writer of popular Gothic romances and looking at the influence that fairy tales, movies, women's magazines, and a wide range of popular cultural forms have on her attitudes, Atwood opens up the issue of how our beliefs are structured by popular media.

We are born into a language and culture that structures us far more than we structure it. Although we are taught to believe that we are free to choose as individuals what is best for us, in fact the possibilities are stringently limited, not only by our talents and tastes, but also by our class, our race, and our gender. This point is driven home metaphorically when Joan is prevented from dancing as a butterfly in a ballet recital. Joan cannot be a ballet dancer, even though she knows her part perfectly, because who ever heard of a fat ballet dancer? This is the first of a long series of lessons about what a woman, fat or thin, can or cannot do. But in her fantasy life, Joan continues to try to find a role she can perform in public, like Chairman Mao who "was fat but successful and . . . didn't take any shit about it" (168). For a while she thinks of being an opera singer, and she toys with being a medium, like Leda Sprott, but then her Fat Lady fantasies take over. Apart from the role of opera singer, in fact, fat women are offered no roles to play in our society that provide both respect and a good income. As Joan discovers, they are either invisible or far too obvious because they are not sexually attractive to men, and this makes it painfully clear that women's main social function, still, is to be attractive to men. Whatever else women might do is judged as secondary. Even when Joan is slender, she keeps her "performing" — her novel writing — private because she's afraid her husband Arthur might disapprove of what she does for a living. His approval matters more to her than her own belief that she writes good romances (and although reading nothing but romances may be destructive, good ones are certainly not easy to write).

The rigid exclusion of certain people from certain roles hurts everyone. Although Joan's desire to be a fat ballet dancer is perhaps a comic example, female police chiefs, Inuit lawyers, black neurosurgeons, blind concert pianists, and wheelchair-bound computer operators are all scarce because of social restrictions, not because of ability. And even when a minority member does succeed, discrimination persists. As Atwood notes of women writers, no matter how successful, they "are like other women: subject to the same discriminatory laws, encountering the same demeaning attitudes, burdened with the same good reasons for not walking through the park alone after dark" (*Second* 194).

Atwood's interest in how particular cultures form people is found in all her novels, and links her nationalist and her feminist themes. This social moulding may lead to positive or negative effects for individuals, but ultimately it is unavoidable. The narrator of *Cat's Eye* comments:

> The past isn't quaint while you're in it. Only at a safe distance, later, when you can see it as décor, not as the shape your life's been squeezed into. They have Elvis Presley zucchini moulds now: you clamp them around your zucchini while it's young, and as it grows, it's deformed into the shape of Elvis Presley's head. (363–64).

Lady Oracle deals with this issue in a far more complex way than either of the two novels that precede it, grounding Joan's behaviour in her childhood and showing her in a series of relationships that allow a pattern to emerge. Interestingly, Joan's image of her national attachments is of an irrevocable operation or something out of her control:

> I was here, in a beautiful southern landscape, with breezes and old-world charm, but all the time my own country was embedded in my brain, like a metal plate left over from an operation; or rather, like one of those pellets you drop into bowls of water, which expand and turn into garish mineral flowers. If I let it get out of control it would take over my head. There was no sense trying to get away . . . . (311–12)

Canada haunts her just as her mother does, not to mention her fat, and it thus becomes one of the things that she has to deal with, a given, not something that can be avoided or escaped.

What this novel has to teach us then, is not only how our culture makes us, but also how we can come to some understanding of this, and ultimately struggle against those parts of our social moulding that, having been internalized, serve to oppress us. As in all her novels, Atwood is concerned with how we can, like the narrator of *Surfacing*, determine "to refuse to be a victim . . . give up the old belief that I am powerless and because of it nothing I can do will ever hurt anyone" (191). Despite her profound awareness of the odds against anyone's achievement of this goal, Atwood shows us women who do take small, but significant steps towards understanding and taking responsibility for their lives. Atwood's own comment on the difficulty of this refusal on the part of the narrator of *Surfacing* is, "It's nice that she doesn't want to be a victim, but if you examine her situation and her society in the cold light of reason, how is she going to avoid it?" ("Interview" [Sandler] 12). Thus it is important that Atwood's heroines are not depicted as unusual or exemplary, simply because the unusual woman is quite often able to succeed, to become the exception that proves the rule. But Atwood wants the rule changed for ordinary women, too (even airheads!), something that will only happen when women confront the existence of these rules in their own lives, and then move to change them for both themselves and other women. Her attempt to show how the struggle is carried on makes this novel an important one.

When Atwood states, "I believe that fiction writing is the guardian of the moral and ethical sense of the community" (*Second* 346), however, she is not saying that fiction writing must convey a clear-cut and serious political message. In fact, she would maintain that this is what political writing should do: "The aim of propaganda is to convince, and to spur people to action; the aim of writing is to create a plausible and moving imaginative world . . ." (*Second* 203). Although many critics have interpreted Atwood's work from a feminist perspective, it can hardly be argued that *Lady Oracle* conveys a feminist message in any direct way, or indeed that only feminists might find it interesting. Rather, by depicting the life of one woman, even in a comically exaggerated way, it makes some feminist positions comprehensible, although Joan herself probably would find a group of feminists as threatening as she comes to find her Brownie pack ("Ever since Brownies I'd been wary of any group composed entirely of women . . ." [85]).

Although *Lady Oracle* is based on popular romance, it does not, as Joan herself fears her romances might, "exploit the masses, corrupt by distracting, and perpetuate degrading stereotypes of women as helpless and persecuted" (30). It certainly does explain why women might want to read romances "when they were too tired to invent escapes of their own" (31). But *Lady Oracle* provides more than simple escape because it may well change our views on what escape means; as Atwood says, "Reading is . . . a process and it also changes you. You aren't the same person after you've read a particular book as you were before, and you will read the next book, unless both are Harlequin Romances, in a slightly different way" (*Second* 345). The escape proposed for women by romance is always marriage to a good man; *Lady Oracle* shows the dangers of promoting marriage, or indeed any single act, as the solution to complex social problems.

Critical Reception

THE AUTHOR'S COMMENTS

Although authors' statements about their works and their intentions are almost invariably interesting, gaps can (and, alas, usually do) occur between what any human being intends to accomplish and the result. Therefore, Atwood's comments on her work should not be seen as conclusive. Further, Atwood's intentions for *Lady Oracle* changed during the writing. To Linda Sandler she remarks, "*Lady Oracle* was more tragic to begin with — it was going to start with a fake suicide and end with a real one." Traces of this version left even after the revision may account for the feeling of some readers that the novel has a dark layer beneath its comic surface. Atwood also notes to Sandler that

> *Lady Oracle* is the most rewritten of my books and it took about two years to write. *Surfacing* and *Edible Woman* each took six months, approximately, although I'd been thinking about them for a long time before I started writing. With *Lady Oracle* the conception and the writing were much closer together. ("Interview" 14–15)

Lady Oracle does seem more complex than Atwood's two earlier novels, especially in its language, its plot, and its characterization of the heroine.

Atwood also discussed her revisions to the narrative structure of *Lady Oracle* with Geoff Hancock:

> *Lady Oracle* was originally written in the second person. It was written as a letter to Arthur. But I realized I couldn't do that,

because Arthur already knew a lot of the stuff that had happened to him. I would have been in the rather stupid position of having the narrator tell Arther things he already knew. It does end up being a story told to somebody else, but you don't figure out who that person is until the end. It isn't Arthur; it's the guy she beans with the bottle. ("Margaret" 269)

Not every reader is likely to figure out that the audience of Joan's first-person narration is, in fact, not only the reader, but also the reporter, a character in the novel. In fact, the reliability of Joan's story is compromised by her desire to look good in his eyes, since as she tells the story she is also beginning to find him rather attractive.

Atwood's revision here not only makes the narration more plausible, but also changes our sense of Joan's character. A heroine who addresses an abandoned husband in a long interior monologue may appear to be a self-indulgent whiner, or may even seem to hover dangerously close to madness. An early draft of the novel, now held at the University of Toronto's Thomas Fisher Rare Book Library, contains this comment of Joan's, which gives an idea of the hopeless tone of such a narrative stance: "But I should give up this dialogue, which has really been a monologue all along, even when we lived together. It's bad for my health. You can't hear me, you never could, and that being the case what else can this be but one more attempt at self-justification" ("Lady"). By producing the same life's story for the reporter, Atwood reveals a Joan firmly anchored in the present, talking to a live listener, rather than a Joan obsessed by an unhappy past, addressing an imaginary Arthur who isn't even listening. The only article that looks closely at the manuscripts of the novel is Carol Beran's "George, Leda, and a Poured Concrete Balcony," which discusses the change in narration and other issues arising from the novel's revisions. Beran, however, argues that Joan is not speaking to the reporter or any other character in the novel, but to the reader alone.

To Beverley Slopen, Atwood remarks that "Characters have a tendency to be the flip side of the coin — to be what you are afraid of becoming. . . . The reason I don't have an untidy life is that I'm afraid I will have an untidy life" (6). This fear may well account for the novel's horrified fascination with Joan's failure to pay attention to her own behaviour and its possible social and moral consequences.

Atwood notes that "Joan is the most likable of the characters I've written about, although I'm not sure I admire her more. She plays at being the clown because she is afraid she is one" (qtd. in Slopen 7). Joan's cheerful oblivion ultimately appears childlike rather than sinister, leaving most readers feeling that she needs to grow up rather than to be condemned.

REVIEWS, ARTICLES AND SECTIONS OF BOOKS

By the time *Lady Oracle* was published in 1976, Margaret Atwood was well known not only in Canada, but also in the United States and Great Britain. The novel was published and reviewed in all three countries. The majority of reviews were positive, or at least neutral. Yet despite their fairly uniform evaluation, they still can be classified by place of origin. Certainly this would not surprise Atwood, who notes that "*Surfacing* was reviewed in the United States almost exclusively as a feminist or ecological treatise; in Canada it was reviewed almost exclusively as a nationalist one" ("Reply" 340). Neither ecological nor nationalist concerns could so easily be attached to a discussion of *Lady Oracle*, but, nonetheless, American reviews tended to take a more exclusively feminist perspective than Canadian ones, which showed a tendency, even if they did discuss feminist issues, to turn to more local concerns (see, for example, Engel). Thus the novel's uncanny ability to recreate the flavour of a Toronto childhood was often praised by Canadian critics, or its very contemporary allusions to the Canadian arts scene noted. Two reviews written by British critics tended to set the novel into a more exclusively literary context (Brigid Brophy, Jane Miller). Because many of the reviews were very brief or raised issues that have subsequently been dealt with more thoroughly, I comment only on those that are still stimulating (even infuriating) or helpful.

One example of a review that is both infuriating and helpful appeared in the *Globe and Mail*. Probably because of Canadian insecurity about the quality of our critical standards with respect to our best writers, rather than out of dissatisfaction with an earlier positive review by Dennis Duffy, the *Globe* asked Brigid Brophy to review the novel. It is rather an unusual step to have the same book reviewed twice, and Atwood herself suggests in an interview that the

Globe deliberately went in search of a negative review ("Interview" [Struthers] 22–23). Still, publicity is publicity, and Brophy is well known, however terrifying her reputation as a reviewer might be. Described as "a noted British critic" at the top of the review, Brophy, also a novelist, tore *Lady Oracle* apart.

Oddly, although some of her points are completely unfair, this review is worth rereading because Brophy does note accurately the important features of the novel, if only to damn them. She begins by attacking Atwood's attention to detail.

This part of the review seems simply petty. She notes that Atwood can't spell the Italian word for "good day," and points out that Terremoto, the name of the Italian village that serves as the setting for the opening and closing scenes of the novel, means "earthquake," only to sneer that is this is hardly the brilliant satire the blurb on the novel's cover promises. She also notes that Atwood runs the name of the London district of Earl's Court into one word. If these comments embarrassed anyone, it was the novel's editor, not Atwood. This part of the review seems simply to be an attempt by Brophy to cast doubt on Atwood's ability to write about Europe with any accuracy. But of course Atwood isn't interested in writing about Europe.

Brophy doesn't seem to realize that most of the satire is aimed at Canada and Atwood herself. Brophy quotes *Lady Oracle* on the furor surrounding the publication of Joan's book of poetry: "The Globe review called it gnomic and chthonic, right in the same paragraph," and then comments: "Whether the furor is plausible is difficult for a foreigner to judge. Can Canada really be such a cushy billet for writers?" Of course it isn't. To try to decide whether an event in a satiric, comic novel is plausible is like trying to decide whether an episode of *Monty Python's Flying Circus* is plausible. Brophy completely misses the point that this passage is satiric, indeed, complexly so. It does imply that the Canadian audience is so uncritical that the production of a book of bad poetry is enough to make one an overnight sensation. But what might seem simply an attack on the poor taste of Canadian readers, reviewers, and critics is complicated by the fact that Atwood is making fun of the reaction to the publication of her own poetry. (The *Globe* comment seems to suit Atwood's *Procedures for Underground* [1970], but much of the satire is directed at the reaction to another collection, *Power Politics* [1971].) We might be inclined to overlook Brophy's ignorance of the

Canadian literary scene if she hadn't so snootily assumed that to misspell two foreign words practically disqualifies Atwood as a writer. Why should Atwood know minute details about Italy and England when Brophy knows so little about the very writer she is presuming to criticize?

When Brophy turns to the more literary aspects of the novel, she is on territory she is better able to judge, and, in fact, many of her points are similar to those made by other reviewers. She comments that Atwood appears to be demonstrating that Joan "like most human beings, consists of the accreted layers of several personalities. However, as none of them has any very personal characteristics, it makes small difference which layer you're at." She extends this insight to the male characters in the book, commenting that they are as "unpersonalized and inert" as Joan. Barbara Amiel, writing in *Maclean's*, makes much the same point: "the faces underneath are no more interesting than the masks themselves." Sam Solecki finds Joan a "shallow girl" and her male characters either "shadowy" or "extended caricature[s]" (344). I.M. Owen, although he praises the novel for "intelligence and wit," its rich, symbolic texture, and interesting incidents (3), also finds the male characters dull: "Joan's father is intentionally dim; Arthur Foster is meant to be dull; and even the flamboyant Royal Porcupine . . . loses his flamboyance" (5). Katha Pollitt feels that in the novel there is "a large vagueness where human beings are concerned." However, comic characters are frequently flatter than characters in realist novels, and it is possible to argue, as in fact I do below, that this odd flatness of character is the result of our seeing all these people through Joan's eyes. For her to see her friends and family as three-dimensional is impossible, since she doesn't even perceive herself that way.

Brophy notes that Joan's "love affairs follow a pattern in which both partners are . . . waiting for a picaresque plot to be hung on them." Both Brophy and another critic, Herbert Rosengarten, complain about the episodic nature of the plot. Rosengarten remarks that "parts of the action are sometimes very tenuously connected. . . . In life, the cause might be quite obscure or trivial; in fiction, we need to feel that such decisions relate to theme or character, that there is some ℩int . . ." (86). However, as Lucy Freibert makes clear in her article `℩e Artist as Picaro," *Lady Oracle* is not only a parody of the ℩ic romance, but also a kind of picaresque novel. The picaresque is a literary form where, as Freibert puts it, "a protagonist usually of uncertain origins" is "thrust into society early, and left totally dependent on the whims of Fortune," and "cast from one adventure to another" (23). In the picaresque, character development is not particularly important, so if *Lady Oracle* can be seen as a version of the picaresque, then it should be forgiven both its flat characters and its episodic plot. The plot's lack of clear cause and effect can further be grounded in Joan's peculiar belief that just as she can invent and then dismiss whole squads of fictional characters, so she can start a new life, a new plot, with a new lover, any time she likes.

Brophy goes on to talk about the wordiness of Atwood's style in *Lady Oracle*, failing to note that it isn't Atwood's style, but Joan's, since Joan, after all, is the narrator. Joan's style, like her life and her body, "had a tendency to spread, to get flabby, to scroll and festoon like the frame of a baroque mirror, which came from following the line of least resistance" (3). Robert Cluett's article makes it clear that the style of *Surfacing* is as pared down and terse as its inexpressive narrator. Atwood herself commented in 1976 that "the ... book I set out to write was a kind of antithesis to *Surfacing*, which is very tight and everything in it fits and there's not anything that's out of place and no tangents. .... In *Lady Oracle* I set out to write a book that was all tangents" (qtd. in Rosenberg 112). Brophy's main thrust seems to be that Atwood is careless about detail, lacks control over the "intellectual tone" of the novel, and has no individual style. But surely these are all traits that can be legitimately ascribed to Joan. Similarly, Brophy blames the novel for its "narcissism" when that is precisely the problem Joan is struggling to overcome. In fact, Sharon R. Wilson, in "The Fragmented Self in *Lady Oracle*," analyzes Joan's behaviour in terms of psychoanalytic theories of narcissism, concluding that by the end of the novel Joan has "at last integrated aspects of her separated self" (80).

Notable, still, for its energetic style and strong moral focus is Wilfred Cude's positive review of *Lady Oracle*. Cude praises Atwood for producing a heroine who is so unambiguously "less than [she] should be" ("Bravo" 50). Joan, "her imagination undernourished by a debilitating mental diet ranging from Disney movies to *True Confessions* magazine, leaves behind her a swath of emotionally mangled people in the name of harmless escapism" (45). Joan, Cude argues, is a victim of the "Miss Flegg Syndrome," the desperate avoidance of ugly reality by the substitution of a gaudy or cute fantasy. Cude equates Joan's inability to see those around her "with compassion and insight" with "Canadian spiritual poverty" in general (49): we are all hooked on escapism. Cude, however, like many other reviewers, assumes that Atwood is pushing a simple moral dichotomy: to face reality is good, while to escape into a fantasy world of romance is bad. But to expect a writer who spends her life manipulating the counters of romance to agree to this seems a little naïve. We all live in a fantasy world of some sort: reality, ugly or beautiful, is only accessible to us through the profoundly ambiguous medium of language. So, ultimately, the cause of Joan's moral failures is not that she does not confront reality, but that she is hooked on impoverished mass fantasies, and reads the complex novel of the world in a simplistic way. However, Cude resembles Joan in believing that everything is clearly bad or good, as in his insistence that good writing should espouse a clear moral stance.

Perhaps because the first step in understanding any novel is to try to make sense of it as a whole, the majority of early articles or sections of books about *Lady Oracle* are general overviews. Naturally enough these tend to overlap, since certain important features of any novel will have to be covered in an overview. Arnold and Cathy Davidson, in "Margaret Atwood's *Lady Oracle*: The Artist as Escapist and Seer," outline the relationship between Joan's self-created victimhood and the effect of the romances she both reads and writes. Clara Thomas's "*Lady Oracle*: The Narrative of the Fool-Heroine," although focusing on Joan as clown, provides a good introduction to an understanding of both the narrative and the novel's implausible plots. Sherrill Grace's chapter in *Violent Duality* is helpful, although somewhat outdated. Ildikó de Papp Carrington's study focuses on the "metaphors of costumes, dancers, and mazes" (68), covering most of the complex issues raised in the novel in an admirably clear and condensed prose.

Several reviews and articles founder, not surprisingly, while trying to elucidate the tricky relationship between reality and fantasy in the novel. Those that assume a simple division between the two regions either oversimplify, like Cude (whose article "Nobody Dunit: The Loose End as Structural Element in *Lady Oracle*" amplifies the point made in his earlier review), or lapse into confusion. Susan Maclean's "*Lady Oracle*: The Art of Reality and the Reality of Art" roams from interesting point to interesting point, frequently commenting on how puzzling and complex the novel is, leaving the reader to follow behind trying to connect the argument. Maclean asks the right questions — "can fiction write the life of the author? Is it through literature that we make ourselves real? Is identity to be found only in fiction and fantasies?" (194) — but fails to venture any answers. Similar problems dog Barbara Rigney's "The 'Escape Artist': *Lady Oracle*," which sees the novel as a lesson on how art can be misused to escape the responsibilities and commitments demanded by reality. For Rigney, Joan's failure can be summed up straightforwardly: "Truth does not translate into art nor art into truth for Joan, as Atwood always indicates that it must" (79). However, although Rigney raises many interesting issues in this article, she never demonstrates how Atwood makes the relationship of truth and art so clear.

Robert Lecker's "Janus through the Looking Glass: Atwood's First Three Novels" was the first to grapple with the interrelationship of reality and fantasy, arguing that although Atwood uses all the literary trappings of the quest for self, Joan is "the victim of a world in which the traditional faith in identity no longer holds" (193), a world where "reality and fantasy are one, and to believe that it is possible to escape from either is the greatest delusion" (198). In his view, those critics who devote themselves to discussing whether Joan has or has not achieved a satisfactory identity or whether she has or has not learned to distinguish reality from fantasy have missed Atwood's point. Thus, instead of seeing the ambiguity of Atwood's ending as most critics have — as a challenge to our interpretive ingenuity, an attempt to make us guess whether Joan has found herself or not — Lecker sees it as a tragic revelation of the disconnected and multiple nature of contemporary life. Some, notably Barbara Godard in her article "My (m)Other, My Self: Strategies for Subversion in Atwood and Hébert," Molly Hite in "Other Side, Other Woman: *Lady Oracle*" and Jessie Givner in "Mirror Images in Margaret Atwood's *Lady Oracle*," would agree with all but Lecker's classification of this vision as tragic, instead seeing the revelation of multiplicity as liberating, since the accepted routes to a satisfactory identity in our culture have always been laid down by powerful white men. Women's inability to find a clearcut independence or identity may thus be seen in a more positive light, as the result of their close emotional ties to others, an' their dependence on the interconnections of community.

Several articles use contemporary feminist psychology to connect Joan's unhappy relationship with her mother with her escapism. Godard's article, "My (m)Other, My Self," draws not only on American feminist criticism, but also on French feminist theory. Her approach to the large number of allusions in the novel (to myth, to fairy tales, and to romance), relates these not just to individual female psychology, but to the social world, a world that is composed of texts. Sue Ann Johnston's "The Daughter as Escape Artist" connects Joan's battle over food and appearance with her mother to Joan's subsequent relationships: "This conflict drives the daughter constantly to seek security and long for freedom. With her husband and lovers Joan feels the same impulse to escape that she once did with her mother" (16). Roberta Rubenstein's *Boundaries of the Self: Gender, Culture, Fiction*, contains an essay, "Escape Artists and Split Personalities," that deals with all of Atwood's novels except *Cat's Eye*. She too examines Joan's relationship with her mother, focusing on Joan's "ambivalent 'bondage' to her mother and her need to escape or separate from her" (77). Judith A. Spector's focus is mainly on the mother-daughter relationship and on feminist issues, but she connects both Joan and her mother to a large number of real and literary *femmes fatales*. Pamela Bromberg's "The Two Faces of the Mirror in *The Edible Woman* and *Lady Oracle*" concentrates on many of the same issues, with added attention given to the cultural requirement that feminine beauty be confirmed by the male gaze. Although several of these studies comment on the issue not only of the mother, but also of the Great Mother, the Triple Goddess of mythology, Roberta Sciff-Zamara's "The Re/Membering of the Female Power in *Lady Oracle*" takes this figure as her focus. Marilyn Patton's "*Lady Oracle*: The Politics of the Body" studies the Goddess in the context of Atwood's working notes for the novel and of her long-standing fascination with Robert Graves's *The White Goddess*. She connects Joan's struggle with the muse, concluding that Atwood "both destroys the Goddess (parodies her, makes her trivial) and celebrates her oracular powers, the force of her language" (46). Two critics, Jane Rule and Rowland Smith, both writing in the 1977 special issue of the *Malahat Review* on Atwood's writing, see Joan's escapism more simply than do the critics discussed above, as a reaction to the stultifying banality of domestic life in Toronto.

Of the other narrowly focused articles, several deal with the issue of genre, trying to establish what kind of novel *Lady Oracle* is: comic, Künstlerroman (novel about the development of an artist), Bildungsroman (novel of education), picaresque, Gothic. Freibert discusses the novel as a version of the picaresque, Grace Stewart deals with it as a version of Künstlerroman, and Frank Davey examines the issue of comedy. Kenneth Hoeppner looks at the novel in terms of Northrop Frye's definition of romance. The majority of critics interested in genre deal with the novel's Gothic elements, and thus their work usually has a feminist element. Susan Rosowski examines the ways Atwood shows contemporary social mythology and Gothic conventions interacting to entrap characters such as Joan. Sybil Korff Vincent, in "The Mirror and the Cameo: Margaret Atwood's Comic/ Gothic Novel, *Lady Oracle*," not only analyzes Atwood's novel, but also suggests that the comic-Gothic may become a new variant of the Gothic, its horror tempered by a contemporary opening up of possibilities for women. Ann McMillan connects the novel to the Gothic tradition in general. She also connects this tradition to contemporary theories of gender relations in several ways, commenting that "Women's victimization and men's exploitation propel one another" (49).

Several articles examine the novel's connections with other works of literature, ranging from myths and fairy tales to Canadian novels by women. Catherine Sheldrick Ross, in "Calling Back the Ghost of the Old-Time Heroine: Duncan, Montgomery, Atwood, Laurence and Munro," points out some fascinating parallels between *Lady Oracle* and L.M. Montgomery's *Anne of Green Gables*, especially those to do with the heroine's immersion in the conventions of romance. Lorraine M. York's "Lives of Joan and Del" compares the heroines' transformations in Alice Munro's *Lives of Girls and Women* and in *Lady Oracle* by examining the novels in the context of Tennyson's poetry, notably *The Princess*, "Mariana," and "The Lady of Shalott." In another paper, "'Banished to this Other Place': Atwood's *Lady Oracle*," Ross, while dealing with the art-life dichotomy in the novel, traces many literary allusions, including those to Lewis Carroll's *Alice through the Looking Glass*. Roslyn Belkin's "The Worth of the Shadow: Margaret Atwood's *Lady Oracle*" explicates the humour in *Lady Oracle* with reference to the writings of Luigi Pirandello. Emily Jensen's "Margaret Atwood's *Lady Oracle*:

A Modern Parable" sees Joan's need for male approval as the heart of her difficulties, noting that many of the allusions in the novel to fairy tales or movies refer to situations where a woman is forced to choose between pleasing men or fulfilling herself artistically. This extremely helpful analysis informs some of the discussion of allusions below. Jensen flounders only as she argues that Joan comes very close to "the victory of knowing that . . . dependency on the approval of others is self-defeating" (45). This occurs when Joan resolves that "From now on . . . I would dance for no one but myself" (*Lady* 335). When Joan dances her adult version of the "Butterfly Frolic" on the Terremoto balcony, however, she ends up cutting her bare feet, ruining, in Jensen's view, "a brilliant scene that could have marked a metaphoric conclusion to the novel and a marvellous triumph for Joan" (45). For Atwood, however, individuals are embedded in a society that renders dependency, whether on a lover, on friends, or on an audience, inevitable; this dependency, as long as it is reciprocal, is rewarding. Since she feels an artist needs a real, not an internalized audience, in her view it would be very difficult to perform for no one but oneself: "I feel that there is a real connection between what gets written and the poet's idea of who she is talking to — and though you may be writing for the ideal reader in the sky, it matters who is down here on earth reacting to the results" (Atwood, "My Craft" 162). As a logical conclusion to the process of situating Atwood's work into the context of other writing comes Judith McCombs' "Atwood's Fictive Portraits of the Artist: From Victim to Surfacer, from Oracle to Birth" which situates *Lady Oracle* into the context of Atwood's entire *oeuvre*, especially with respect to the delineation of the woman as artist.

To date, the critics have used feminist psychology, theories of literary genre, ideas of the relation between fantasy and reality, and the study of allusions to myth, popular culture, and literature to illuminate Atwood's novel. Few articles examine Atwood's political, moral, or philosophical attitudes very closely, however. Most critics appear to assume, like Cude, that Atwood shares their own values (and in some cases, of course, they may be right). As a result, there is a blind spot in the criticism, similar to the blind spot in the American feminist critiques that generally see Atwood in terms of her female contemporaries in the United States, while ignoring her nationalist views. However, Atwood has been examined from positions other than liberal feminist ones and these examinations, whatever one thinks of their validity, are always interesting. W.J. Keith, for example, says that Atwood is perhaps more traditional and less radical than many critics assume. Larry MacDonald makes a similar point from much farther to the left than does Keith. Beryl Langer, as a Marxist critic, is interested, not in pinning down Atwood's personal political views, but in showing how her themes, characters, and narrative strategies can be related to the economic and class features of late capitalism.

Because Atwood is such a popular writer, those aspects of her work that concern us on a first reading have so far dominated the criticism. Atwood tends to downplay her own scholarly accomplishments, but someone who has completed almost all the requirements for a Harvard doctorate might well be suspected of considerable depth of thought and wide-ranging literary knowledge. Although, as Joan herself notes, surfaces are important, perhaps it is time to pay attention to Atwood's considerable depth.

Reading of the Text

THE ROMAN À CLEF AND THE
SATIRE OF CANADIAN CULTURE

A roman à clef is a novel in which real people appear in fictional guises thin enough to be penetrated, if not by everyone, at least by those who know their milieu and that of the author. *Lady Oracle* was quickly labelled a roman à clef in the Canadian reviews, Patricia Morley remarking, for example, "To add to the fun, some of the characters whom Joan encounters will be recognizable to the Canadian literary world" (49). Although Morley implies that recognizing these characters is rather unimportant, Atwood is not simply telling in-jokes. Like the literary allusions to myth, popular culture, and fairy tale, these contemporary references often add depth to the novel's meaning.

The roman à clef issue was brought up in most detail in *Saturday Night* for November 1976. Robert Fulford, the editor, pointed out that some of the satire seemed to be directed at left-wing nationalists such as Atwood herself. Like Brophy, Fulford cannot really understand someone who would engage in self-satire, even though its close relative, self-deprecation, is supposed to be a Canadian national habit. He notes that Atwood, in *This Magazine*, a nationalist magazine "possibly not unlike *Resurgence*" (which Joan's husband, Arthur, edits in the novel), had attacked Mordecai Richler's satire of Canadian nationalism and nationalists in *The Incomparable Atuk*. (Atwood's attack is delivered in "What's So Funny?", an essay reprinted in her *Second Words*). Fulford remarks that "She made it chillingly clear that she regarded this kind of satire as proof of sick self-hatred." He suggests then that the satire in *Lady Oracle* reveals that Atwood has abandoned nationalism, and implies rather snidely that she has done so because she finds it insufficiently trendy. However, Atwood's subsequent involvement in such nationalist projects as the publication of the anti-free trade book, *If You Love This Country* (1987), indicates that she is still as nationalist as ever. Certainly the implication of Joan's attack on Arthur and his cell, the diatribe that leads to the plan to bomb the Peace Bridge, is that nationalism can be praiseworthy and effective in some cases and silly or destructive in others: hardly an extreme position. She cannot agree with Richler, then, because his satire is aimed at all nationalism. Nonetheless, critics other than Fulford have also been puzzled by Atwood's political satire here. Larry MacDonald has said that Atwood's inability to see any solution coming out of political organization or community effort (he comments on Arthur's career) is the result of her inability to see beyond liberal values: "If Atwood did not want to trivialize the rich and challenging tradition of socialist and nationalist thought and action, she would not always choose to embody it in narcissistic fools who are philosophical and political illiterates" (133).

Atwood, ignoring Fulford's comment on her nationalism altogether, remarked, in a letter published in the next issue of *Saturday Night*, "I was . . . shocked by the implication that I myself write *romans à clef*. I neither write them nor approve of them" ("Royal"). She continues to say that she did not, as had been suggested, model the Royal Porcupine after the writer Doug Fetherling. She goes on to add that the Royal Porcupine was not modelled after several other people: Charles Pachter (an artist), Mark Prent (a sculptor), Dr. Brute (Eric W. Metcalfe, a painter and performance artist), bill bissett (a poet whose book, *Nobody Owns th Earth*, was edited by Atwood and Dennis Lee), or Flakey Rose Hips (a pseudonym for Glenn Lewis, an artist). Since *Saturday Night* had not even mentioned these people, speculation had obviously been widespread. Her style in this letter is as inflated and thus as untrustworthy as that of the novel, however. In an interview with J.R. (Tim) Struthers, she is more forthcoming, saying "I made up that whole thing about the Royal Porcupine, you know, that whole scenario," but confessing that she had two contemporary artists in mind, one being Mark Prent, and another (whose name she couldn't remember) "who covers everything in fur" (26).

Atwood herself is an artist as well as a writer. Since 1975, under the pen name Bart Gerrard, she has been drawing cartoons (*Kanadian*

Kultchur Komix) for *This Magazine*, featuring "Survivalwoman," who wears snowshoes and lives in the Bloor Street Viaduct. She did the illustrations for her collection of poems, *The Journals of Susanna Moodie* (1970), and for some of her other works; some of her watercolours are housed in the University of Toronto's Thomas Fisher Rare Book Library. The Royal Porcupine is only one of the many characters in her writing that are artists of one kind or another. That many of her allusions are to the Canadian art scene, then, is hardly surprising.

Atwood frequently seizes on contemporary details of this scene that fit her novelistic needs perfectly. On the verge of her first promotion tour, Joan thinks of other public figures, including Mr. Peanut "who would come to the Loblaws parking lot on special Saturdays. . . . As a child I'd loved him, but suddenly I saw what it was like to be the peanut: clumsy, visible and suffocating" (235). As she finds during her mothball dance, the limelight is not always rewarding if one's serious aspirations are consistently misunderstood and trivialized. The media quickly construct a version of her that she doesn't recognize. This phenomenon was the subject of the performance art of Vincent Trasov, whose work for five years consisted of dressing up as a peanut. He ran, as Mr. Peanut, for Mayor of Vancouver in 1974. Trasov made two points (at least): that images, rather than real people, run for public office, and that artists are allowed few powerful roles to play in Canada, instead being treated as idiosyncratic members of a self-indulgent fringe group. Atwood's attacks on the media's tendency to misinterpret, to sensationalize, and to create distorted personae for well-known writers are found in many of her interviews and articles: "*What is Hard to Find* is an interviewer who regards writing as a respectable profession, not as some kind of magic, madness, trickery or evasive disguise for a Message; and who regards an author as someone engaged in a professional activity" (*Second* 201–02).

The novel's most colourful character, the Royal Porcupine, aroused the most speculation. Although, as Atwood herself says, he is modelled on no single person, he has elements of several poets and artists who are contemporaries of Atwood. All have been subjected to various degrees of misunderstanding, in some cases leading to calls for public condemnation, the withdrawal of Canada Council support, and even censorship. bill bissett aroused public ire for a poem he wrote praising the importance of "a warm place to shit." Glenn Lewis commented on the problem of artistic identity by taking photographs of himself, in his role as "Flakey Rose Hips," dressed up as Hitler. Eric Metcalfe paints under a pseudonym. Like the Royal Porcupine, Metcalfe, Lewis, and Trasov all play with identities and roles. However, the work of two other artists, Charles Pachter and Mark Prent, seems even more relevant in considering that of the Royal Porcupine.

Charles Pachter has been a friend of Atwood's since they were both counsellors at Camp White Pine in 1958; he produced illustrations for special editions of her poetry and did the portrait that is reproduced on the dust jacket of *Second Words*. (And to say that the Porcupine resembles him in some ways does not mean that we have to believe that Pachter and Atwood carried on a passionate affair while hauling dead animals around Toronto in garbage bags.) Pachter is well known for his painting of the queen saluting from the back of a moose, one of a series on the queen (or the moose) done in 1972, called variously "Monarchs of the North" or "Homage to the Colonial Mentality" (see Aspinall). His artistic sense of humour, a cross between the irreverent and the patriotic, certainly resembles the Royal Porcupine's (whose name itself seems to point to those royal moose rides). Unlike the Porcupine, however, Pachter showed enough ambivalence toward the queen to arouse the ire of Canadian monarchists. Pachter was also part of a co-op gallery that ran *The Ugly Show*, where artists of all degrees of fame were invited to display the worst art they had either created or discovered. This may have given Atwood her idea for the journal that Fraser Buchanan supposedly once edited, "a literary magazine called *Reject*; the idea was that it would print only stuff that'd been rejected by other literary magazines" (*Lady* 260). Indeed, Buchanan resembles the editor of a small literary review, *Northern Journey*, that published a few issues in the 1970s.

Mark Prent's art caused a good deal of controversy in the early 1970s. His *And Is There Anything Else You'd Like, Madam*, consisted of a butcher's display case filled with neat trays of realistic imitation human body parts, plastic price stickers attached. His *Five Stuffed Crows* depicted the birds' attack on a mangled human body. Reaction to these images is horror and disgust, although we do not always feel this when we walk into the reality of a butcher's shop, whiz past flattened animals on the highway, or see stuffed crows in an art gallery, for that matter. Prent's point is, as Michael Greenwood notes in *Artscanada* in 1972, that

> If the outrage of cannibalism seems so much more atrocious than the sanctioned outlets for human violence to which we have become morally anaesthetized, we may begin to reflect seriously upon the root causes of human aggression and our failure to divert them into constructive channels. (40)

Yet some people reacted to these works as if Prent was advocating cannibalism, instead of seeing the protest against our cultural numbness about the destruction we inflict on animals. Similarly, protesters picket the Royal Porcupine's display of frozen, dead animals as if he had killed them himself; that his art might also be protesting the destruction of nature by technology doesn't seem to occur to anyone (even himself, I might add!). This scene is also an allusion to *Survival*, where Atwood suggests that Canadians identify with animal victims because of "a deep-seated cultural fear": "And for the Canadian animal, bare survival is the main aim in life, failure as an individual is inevitable, and extinction as a species is a distinct possibility" (*Survival* 79).

Her example of how the Royal Porcupine's art is wildly misinterpreted is just one of many in the novel, and is part of a larger commentary on the complex relationship between the artist, reality, and art, a relationship that appears to be doomed to misunderstanding by reviewers, interviewers, critics, and the general public.

Although Atwood justifiably becomes annoyed when her readers confuse her with her heroines ("how did she lose all that weight?"), enough hints are dropped to inspire any reader to try to make some sort of connection between Atwood's life and the novel. Since Joan is obviously an inflated, comic figure, to try to work out a consistent biographical equation would be a mistake. But the sections that deal with Joan's writing career almost beg to be interpreted through Atwood's own. Perhaps the most obvious connection is that between Joan's book of poems, *Lady Oracle*, and Atwood's poetry collection *Power Politics* (1971), published by House of Anansi Press. Both books deal with male-female relations, and both were assumed to be about the poet's marriage. Black Widow Press (which rejects Joan's poetry as schlock) is clearly intended to be a comic version of House of Anansi, just as the publisher Morton and Sturgess is a comic version of the publishers McClelland and Stewart. Atwood became a member of the editorial board at Anansi (named after the African trickster figure, a spider) in 1971. Morton and Sturgess's eagerness to accept Joan's poetry (described as a cross between Rod McKuen and Kahlil Gibran — that is, sentimental and quasi-mystical) might be seen as an attack on the real publishers until we realize that they published Atwood's *Lady Oracle* as well as Joan's. Again, Atwood thwarts a simplistic reading.

Although all the trivialization of artists perpetrated by the media may seem exactly that — trivial — Atwood's main point in the novel is that Joan's concept of what women should aspire to is limited by those stereotypes that form the currency of the popular media. In her essay "On Being a Woman Writer," Atwood describes some of the stereotypes that have been applied to her: "Happy Housewife," "Ophelia," "Miss Martyr," and "Miss Message" (*Second* 200–01). Joan converts her mother into a monster when she is about seven years old; the media convert Joan into one in the adult world, live on daytime television. The media generally thrive on the extremist thinking that Atwood describes as Gothic, and require that complicated human beings fit into their simplistic hero/villain pattern, thus perpetuating simplistic thinking in readers, listeners, and viewers. Certainly Joan's return to Toronto will instantly deflate her public image and frustrate the death cultists, although the media will likely respond by producing another badly distorted version of her.

Running through the satire found in the roman à clef allusions is a critique of simplistic, sensationalist, and knee-jerk reactions to art. This critique is also found in the more obvious themes of the novel, especially in Joan's refusal to look critically at the Gothic tradition in which she herself works.

JOAN'S IDENTITY

Atwood's heroines tend to suffer identity crises, often appearing to lack clear-cut personalities, opinions, or tastes. (One metaphor for this problem is their difficulty in choosing, or at times even wearing clothes, or choosing, or at times even eating food.) Joan, however, as her high-school yearbook notes, has a "terrific personality" (91). And, in rebelling against her mother's style, sterile and conformist, Joan does develop an extremist style that she calls "baroque" (3). Jorge Borges calls this a style "which deliberately exhausts (or tries to exhaust) its possibilities and borders on its own caricature" (qtd. in Irby xxii).

Just as her child self tried to eat everything, so her style tries to incorporate everything and becomes inflated and ridiculous. When she cries, for example, "The grief was always real but it came out as a burlesque of grief, an overblown imitation . . ." (6). She tries to repress this style in public, except in the gaudy (and later romantic) clothes she wears. She herself comes close to realizing that she didn't choose this style freely, but developed it as a reaction to her mother; she thinks, "I was not her puppet; surely I was behaving like this not because of anything she had done but because I wanted to" (86). To a large degree, however, as children, we are our parents' puppets, as Peter Berger and Thomas Luckmann point out in *The Social Construction of Reality*:

> One must make do with the parents that fate has regaled one with. This unfair disadvantage in the situation of being a child has the obvious consequence that, although the child is not simply passive in the process of his socialization, it is the adults who set the rules of the game. The child can play the game with enthusiasm or with sullen resistance. But, alas, there is no other game around. (154)

However, that Joan chooses to resist, even passively, rather than to play along, is evidence of some strength of character.

Stuck with unloving parents, Joan nonetheless feels that once she loses weight and leaves home she can fabricate a new self. Instead of telling her lovers about her past, she makes up a more normal childhood, as if by rewriting personal history she can also abolish it and substitute a new and preferable one (see Rule). The concept of an inner true self just waiting to be discovered, like the thin body Joan discovers after her diet, is false, however, as her inability to lose her mental image of the fat self reveals. No one who lives in a human culture can remain without an identity (however fragmented) to the age of 19, when Joan leaves home. If she has a true self, it is inextricably linked to the fat little girl who dreamed of being a ballet dancer, as the grownup Joan's recurrent Fat Lady fantasies prove. Her belief that her new physical appearance means that she can start a similarly new emotional life is equally mistaken. Joan sometimes seems to believe that our identities are completely determined by our parents and our culture, and that thus we are, in Atwood's terms, victims. Therefore she frequently depicts herself as unable to take responsibility for her behaviour. Sometimes she moves to the other extreme, apparently believing that she can make up her own identity, regardless of her past, just as she composes the identities of her fictional characters. This view of the individual as "self-made" is a powerful one in our culture. But, in fact, as with most of the dualisms Atwood presents, the reality is somewhere in between the two extremes. We do, to a certain degree, construct our own identities, but we have to work with the materials made available to us by our past and our culture. Further, identity is not formed once and for all in childhood, or at any other stage of growth, but is constantly revised and reformulated in reaction to social forces. To believe otherwise is to believe in fixed identities, a belief that supports the stereotyping of ourselves and others. Society offers individuals a finite set of roles and a few patterns of acceptable behaviour, and we choose those that seem to our child selves most pleasurable or, at least, most conducive to emotional survival. Certainly destructive behaviour patterns chosen by our child selves under duress can later be confronted and changed, but only with considerable effort. Joan's habits of eavesdropping, overeating, overreacting, and paying more attention to what others think than thinking for herself, persist — evidence that starting over is difficult, if not impossible. Most significantly, Joan's typical response — to ignore, deny, or escape, rather than to confront — survives, leading to the novel's ridiculous plot.

Surviving Childhood

Although Joan realizes that her mother and her father (and later her husband, Arthur) are not particularly loving, she can't articulate the problem clearly enough to escape the effects of their self-centred unhappiness. Nonetheless, she has discovered tactics to cope with the lack of emotional warmth in her family. That these are tactics, rather than the inevitable result of her parents' coldness is clear because she shifts easily from one persona to another depending on her context: "At home I was sullen or comatose, at the movies I wept with Aunt Lou, but at school I was doggedly friendly and outgoing" (91). At home, she is unfriendly, but she refuses to be unobtrusive:

> I had developed the habit of clomping silently but very visibly through rooms in which my mother was sitting; it was a sort of fashion show in reverse, it was a display, I wanted her to see and recognize what little effect her nagging and pleas were having. (68–69)

This is a power struggle, and ultimately Joan wins by reducing her mother to tears, driving her to drink, and goading her into extremist measures. It may be a destructive, unpleasant, and boring game, but it is a game, and both play it as if their lives depended on it (see Berne). At school, Joan works to fit in with equal fervour, concealing her own needs in order to get as much attention as one so fat can hope for. Even after the fat goes away, she retains this tactic.

Joan's Denial of Self

Outside her family circle, Joan tries to get attention by being unobtrusive: "I was a sponge, I drank it all in but gave nothing out" (93). She wants attention, but doesn't want anyone to look at her too closely, because she fears rejection, especially of her fat and embarrassing child self. Thus, paradoxically, she decides that the only way to get any attention is to efface herself: to be invisible. Thus, she becomes frantic every time she encounters someone from her former life. When she discovers that Eunice P. Revele, the woman who is to marry her and Arthur, is Leda Sprott, the spiritualist medium who ran the séances her aunt took her to as a child, she panics: "She looked me straight in the face, and I could tell she knew exactly who I was. I moaned and closed my eyes" (203). When she begs Revele not to tell Arthur about her shape ("I couldn't say 'fat'; I used that word about myself only in my head" [208]), the medium is amused. When

Joan meets one of the Brownies who used to torment her, she flees into the nearest washroom to cry. Her behaviour seems ridiculous, but it shows the fear she has of facing her own behaviour and her own history. Although she had the courage as a child to defy her mother, as an adult she seems, at least in public, to have become a panic-stricken conformist, following all the advice given out by women's magazines on hooking a man through self-effacement. She was not prepared to pay the price of conformity to her mother's will in order to get her mother's love, but she is prepared to pay almost anything to buy the love of a man. This perhaps is evidence that Joan did understand one thing her mother was trying to convey: society regards the love of a man as crucial for women; the love of other women is dispensable.

Once Joan has left home, she tries to construct a new self. Losing weight is like being reborn: "I was now a different person, and it was like being born fully grown at the age of nineteen: I was the right shape, but I had the wrong past. I'd have to get rid of it entirely and construct a different one for myself, a more agreeable one" (141). When Arthur asks her about a picture of her fat past self, she claims it is her Aunt Deirdre: "It hurt me a little to betray myself like that. The picture was an opening and I should have taken it, it was still early enough for such risks. Instead I retreated behind the camouflage of myself as Arthur perceived me" (90). Here it is clear that Joan knows she has a self, and calls it "I," but she keeps this self behind a mask that she has constructed to please others. She is afraid that if she reveals her "real self" others will reject her: "But if [Arthur'd] known what I was really like, would he still have loved me?" (33). Thus she disguises her odd past and her peculiar fantasies so that they will be unrecognizable, publishing them as Gothic romances under an assumed name. Even when she publishes her poetry, she never discusses it with Arthur. Her identity, childhood, and creativity all are repressed.

For Joan, to reveal herself is always dangerous: "In my experience, honesty and expressing your feelings could lead to only one thing. Disaster" (33). She is afraid of recognition because she sees this as "unmasking" and she is ashamed of what she believes to be her "real" self. Her adult social "mask" is so bland, so socially acceptable, that it is a kind of camouflage, just as her fat once was. Thus, oddly, despite her fears of being recognized, she often behaves as if she is invisible.

Her fat formerly acted as a "magic cloak of blubber and invisibility" (141), which turned her into an onlooker, and she still retains the sense that she is invisible even after she has become, in fact, a highly visible public figure, with distinctive long red hair. In Terremoto, where she hides after her faked suicide, she seems incapable of realizing that the villagers will remember her from the time she spent there with Arthur the year before. When it dawns on her that they might, she is surprised: "It's no good thinking you're invisible if you aren't, and the problem was: if I had recognized the old man, perhaps he had recognized me" (8). Her reaction to this insight is to hack off her red hair and to dye what is left, forgetting that the villagers are bound to notice the change. Only at the end of the novel does she realize why they have been looking at her so strangely; as her landlord explains:

"People talk of this," he said finally. "They do not understand why you have put your clothes beneath the house. They know of this. They do not know why you have cut off your so beautiful hair, that everyone remembers from the time you are here before, with your husband. . . ." (326)

What appears to be colossal stupidity here is, in fact, a revelation of her belief that she does not really exist, does not really have a self, even though she very obviously does. (One metaphoric proof of this is the return of her buried clothes, "neatly washed and pressed," by Mr. Vitroni, her landlord [326].) Although she believes everyone is out to get her, she simultaneously believes that no one can see her: in fact, the first belief is a way of compensating for the second. Similarly, her enormous insecurity about what others will think about her leads to attempts at self-concealment; her hunger for love and recognition drives her in the opposite direction. When she is fat, she is, as she notes, "a huge featureless blur. If I'd ever robbed a bank no witness would have been able to describe me accurately" (80). To compensate, she buys outrageously gaudy clothes: "I wasn't going to let myself be diminished, neutralized, by a navy-blue polka-dot sack" (85). Similarly, when she loses weight, the need for dramatic self-expression at first goes inward, into the composition of Gothic romances under an assumed name, but finally erupts in the publication of her poetry and her affair with the Royal Porcupine.

Despite the novel's comic tone, Atwood takes care to make Joan's odd behaviour psychologically plausible. Neither of Joan's parents is capable of providing her with ordinary human warmth. Joan's early fantasy that she isn't really her mother's daughter, but Aunt Lou's, breaks down when she asks herself: "what could have persuaded my mother to take me in if she hadn't been obliged to" (87). She and her father never talk: "I kept waiting for him to give me some advice, warn me, instruct me, but he never did any of these things. Perhaps he felt as if I weren't really his daughter . . ." (74–75). Joan asks herself: "Why did they both act as though he owed my mother something?" The answer comes as Joan eavesdrops on her parents' fights in the kitchen by putting her "head into the toilet" and "listen[ing] to them through the pipes." What she hears is her mother saying "It's not as though I wanted to have her. It's not as though I wanted to marry you. I had to make the best of a bad job if you ask me." Apparently, Joan's mother got pregnant by accident, and worse, had asked Joan's father to abort Joan: "You're a doctor, don't tell me you couldn't have done something" (75).

Joan tries to figure out what she meant, but can't, at the conscious level, at least, "and when she'd say, 'If it wasn't for me you wouldn't be here,' *I didn't believe her*" (76; emphasis added). Joan eats in response: "Sometimes I was afraid I wasn't really there, I was an accident; I'd heard her call me an accident. . . . Had I trapped my father, if he really was my father, had I ruined my mother's life? I didn't dare to ask" (76). No wonder Joan feels simultaneously both angry and guilty. Her eating is done partly to vent her anger at her mother's failure to nurture her, and partly to compensate for it. Instead of withering away, or becoming the perfect slender clone her mother wants, Joan takes over the task of nurturing herself. She builds up her body around her, a comforting mass of flesh, a pseudowomb, an enormous breast.

Evidence to support what might at first seem a rather strange suggestion can be found in the novel. When the boy that Joan's schoolmate Valerie rejects flings his arms around Joan's stomach, her retrospective comment is, "he might have perceived me as a single enormous breast" (97). By this time, she is not only nurturing herself, but others, listening sympathetically to the girls at school, and she remains not only a good eavesdropper but also a good listener. Later, when she and Arthur are in Italy, they visit Tivoli and see a statue of Diana of Ephesus: "She had a serene face, perched on top of a body shaped like a mound of grapes. She was draped in breasts from neck to ankle. . . . Once I would have seen her as an image of myself, but not any more. My ability to give was limited, I was not inexhaustible" (255). At this point, Joan is making a last attempt to salvage her marriage, but clearly her desire to suppress her need for recognition is on the wane.

In one sense, Joan's "decision" to "become her own mother" shows great strength. It allows her to act like a sensible and supportive parent when others come to her for emotional support. But this strategy leaves part of her still unsatisfied:

> What [Arthur] didn't know was that behind my compassionate smile was a set of tightly clenched teeth, and behind that a legion of voices, crying, *What about me? What about my own pain? When is it my turn?* But I'd learned to stifle these voices, to be calm and receptive. (90)

The fat that helped her survive childhood is a defence that she needs to come to terms with rather than ignore, since the habits that it represents increasingly interfere with her finding happiness for herself. Worse, her fat still haunts her, since it represents a part of herself she has tried to kill:

> When I looked at myself in the mirror, I didn't see what Arthur saw. The outline of my former body still surrounded me, like a mist, like a phantom moon, like the image of Dumbo the Flying Elephant superimposed on my own. I wanted to forget the past, but it refused to forget me; it waited for sleep, then cornered me. (216)

The comic image of Dumbo the Elephant becomes progressively more monstrous. In Terremoto, Joan fantasizes:

> Below me, in the foundations of the house, I could hear the clothes I'd buried there growing themselves a body . . . a creature composed of all the flesh that used to be mine and which must

have gone somewhere. It would have no features, it would be smooth as a potato, pale as starch, it would look like a big thigh, it would have a face like a breast minus the nipple. It was the Fat Lady. She rose into the air and descended on me as I lay stretched out in the chair. . . . Within my former body, I gasped for air. Disguised, concealed, white fur choking my nose and mouth. Obliterated. (322)

These nightmares make Joan's failure to deal with her past fat self clear. And one nightmare gives us the key to her problem:

In the worst dream . . . I would be hiding behind a door, or standing in front of one, it wasn't clear which. It was a white door, like a bathroom door or perhaps a cupboard. I'd been locked in, or out, but on the other side of the door I could hear voices. Sometimes there were a lot of voices, sometimes only two; they were talking about me, discussing me, and as I listened I would realize that something very bad was going to happen. I felt helpless, there was nothing I could do. In the dream I would back into the farthest corner of the cubicle and wedge myself in, press my arms against the walls, dig my heels against the floor. They wouldn't be able to get me out. Then I would hear the footsteps, coming up the stairs and along the hall. (215)

This dream closely resembles the occasions she eavesdrops on her parents in the bathroom, when she discovers that her mother, at least, considered aborting her. And, by analogy, her behaviour can be seen as a refusal, not just to grow up, but even to be born. She remains, at some levels, the helpless foetus cowering in the womb, frightened that her father, turned murderer, is coming to get her out. That abortion is the nightmare at the heart of *Surfacing*, the novel that preceded *Lady Oracle*, gives this point added resonance. Further, as Ildikó de Papp Carrington comments in a discussion of *The Edible Woman*, Atwood has represented characters as foetal before. Carrington remarks that when Duncan and Marian make love, it occurs "between two sexless and nearly dead foetuses" (48). Duncan remarks to Marian in this scene that "Assuming the foetal position won't be any help at all, god knows I've tried it long enough" (*Edible* 254).

Further, Joan's situation in Terremoto is described in terms that make it analogous, not to hell or heaven, but to limbo, the region on the border of hell where unbaptized infants, among others, are sent, because although unqualified for salvation, they don't deserve damnation, either: "I was . . . taking a steamy sunbath in the middle of nowhere. The Other Side was no paradise, it was only a limbo" (311). Her marriage, too, has been a kind of limbo, a kind of womb, where, because she hasn't ever mentioned her mother or her past, she doesn't have to deal with them. She is afraid of bringing her various selves together during her marriage with Arthur:

> Why did I feel I had to be excused? Why did I want to be exempted, and what from? In high school you didn't have to play baseball if you had your period or a pain in your stomach, and I preferred the sidelines. Now I wanted to be acknowledged, but I feared it. . . . Instead I floated, marking time. (218)

She is floating as in the womb because to be born is to become part of culture, to be moulded, to make decisions, to take sides, to sin, to be an adult, and she is afraid of that. Just as the heroine of *Surfacing* attempts to avoid guilt by identifying with animal victims such as the hanged heron, Joan puts herself in the position of another helpless victim, exempt from participation in a game in which one risks winning or losing.

The reward for avoiding guilt by seeing oneself as a helpless victim is that one can escape taking any emotional or moral responsibility for one's acts. The punishment is that one cannot really consciously empower oneself to be creative, loving, or accomplished. The minute one admits one is powerful, one must accept the guilt for the inevitable misuse of that power. The results of refusing to take on either power or responsibility are self-loathing, fear, and the transformation of those perceived as responsible into one-dimensional monsters. Just as the narrator of *Surfacing* blames almost everyone around her for being "American," so Joan ultimately casts her mother as a monster and all the men she knows as villains, because this is the only way to account for her own unhappiness without considering her own contribution to it.

In *Lady Oracle*, Atwood conveys this message in several ways, both major and minor, comic and serious. In a minor example, Joan's typical response is activated by the letters she gets from people who want her advice on getting published:

> When I explained that I had no surefire contacts in the publishing world, they were outraged to be told I was powerless. It overwhelmed me with guilt that I couldn't live up to their expectations, so after a while I started throwing the letters out unanswered, and after that, unread. (251)

When asked for help or support or action, Joan's response is to demonstrate powerlessness and feel terrible guilt at being so weak. When this becomes too painful, she avoids guilt by refusing to take any responsibility. Although perhaps these fans were not likely to be satisfied with any response except instant publication, Joan cannot avoid dealing with any request for a demonstration of power in the same way.

Joan prefers the pretence of powerless innocence to confrontation and possible rejection. To avoid or escape and be ignored or overlooked may be painful but it appears better than being recognized, understood, and rejected. However, as her marriage continues,

> I began to feel something was missing. Perhaps, I thought, I had no soul; I just drifted around, singing vaguely, like the Little Mermaid in the Andersen fairy tale. In order to get a soul you had to suffer, you had to give something up; or was that to get legs and feet? (218)

To get a soul she has to give up pretending she isn't an adult and stand on her own two feet. By the end of the novel she does start to change her escapist habits: she takes responsibility for hitting the reporter and she seems likely to return to Toronto to take responsibility for her "suicide." As so often in Atwood, the fairy tale casts light on Joan's situation, as do several other literary works and stories alluded to in the novel.

"The Little Mermaid," "The Red Shoes," and "The Lady of Shalott"

Although a psychological motive can be found for Joan's withholding her fat past from Arthur, she also seems very concerned to keep her skill at writing Gothic romances from him:

> I longed to marry Arthur, but I couldn't do it unless he knew
> the truth about me and accepted me as I was, past and present.
> He'd have to be told I'd lied to him, that I'd never been a
> cheerleader, that I myself was the fat lady in the picture. I would
> also have to tell him that I'd quit my job as a wig-seller several
> months before and was currently finishing *Love Defied*, on the
> proceeds of which I expected to live for at least the next six
> months. (198)

Her fear seems to be based on the clear message that she has received
throughout her childhood and adolescence that a woman cannot
have both a marriage and a career at the same time. Emily Jensen
traces this message in two Hans Christian Andersen fairy stories,
"The Little Mermaid" and "The Red Shoes," on a 1948 movie based
on the latter story and on Tennyson's poem "The Lady of Shalott."
(The Disney film *The Whale Who Wanted to Sing at the Met* [*Lady
5*] fits into this pattern too, but perhaps we need not go overboard.)
In each, a woman is punished for wanting both to be an artist and to
be loved.

In the Hans Christian Andersen story, the Little Mermaid falls in
love with a prince, and asks a sea witch to give her feet so she can
marry him. The witch does so, but cuts out the mermaid's tongue as
payment. The mermaid's ability to sing has been sacrificed for love.
The witch tells her that if the prince loves her wholeheartedly and
marries her, then she will gain a human soul; otherwise, when he
marries another, her heart will break and she will disappear into foam.
Her love never fails, even when the prince marries someone else, and,
despite the witch's prophecy, the Mermaid receives a soul and goes
to heaven. But she loses both art and love to do so.

The fairy tale "The Red Shoes" is about an orphan who is given a
pair of red shoes that dance her around the countryside, something
she initially enjoys. However, she has to get the public executioner
to cut off her feet in order to stop dancing. Visions of the red shoes
persist, but finally she achieves sufficient piety to resist them. Jensen
comments that "The conflict here is between the girl's love for dance
and the submissive piety demanded by the church" (30). The film
version "with Moira Shearer as a ballet dancer torn between her

career and her husband" was Joan's favourite: "I wanted to dance and be married to a handsome orchestra conductor, both at once — and when she finally threw herself in front of a train I let out a bellowing snort that made people three rows ahead turn around indignantly" (79). Tennyson's poem "The Lady of Shalott" concerns a woman who cannot both weave and love, and whose abandonment, for love, of her world of art and of mirrors ends in death. Atwood has commented on her own early acceptance of this need to choose:

> The only thing I regard as important was the moment I realized I wanted to be a writer. . . . All my early poems were terrible, but that didn't matter. At that time I felt I couldn't get married and have kids and be a writer too. A pretty heavy acknowledgement for a sixteen year old girl. (qtd. in Miner 181)

She notes elsewhere that when the women's liberation movement hove into view, its writers "were assuring me that I didn't have to get married and have children. But what I wanted was someone to tell me I could" ("Great" xvi). Of course, when Joan tries to "dance for no one but [her]self" (335), her cut feet allude to the red shoes and the mermaid's painful feet (The glass on the balcony seems the result of Mr. Vitroni's poor housekeeping, since it is on that balcony, a year earlier, that Arthur and Joan "sit among the pieces of broken glass" [254].)

Joan is like the mermaid before she loves: without a soul. Like the unbaptized babies, she cannot be damned or exalted. Although her tongue has not been cut out, she says nothing to Arthur of any importance. As a good listener, she cannot ever speak about herself. Her Gothic voice is unknown to him, and, significantly, when her book of poems is published, he withdraws from her. Given the importance that her fantasy life places on dancing and on writing, the publication of the book of poetry might well be seen as a twofold breakthrough for Joan. She has finally admitted her creative side to Arthur and she seems to have come into some kind of touch with her inner world. But typically, she avoids taking responsibility for what she contributed to the poems by telling an interviewer that she produced them by practising automatic writing (239), which is only partly true. And she avoids thinking about the images in her poems until long after she has written them.

Lady Oracle *and Archetypal Patterns*

Although Atwood has downplayed the influence of Northrop Frye's ideas on her work (*Second* 400), certainly the archetypal pattern of death and rebirth that he stresses, of descent into the underworld and return with precious knowledge, fits what happens to Joan. Her first descent into the underworld is her descent into the mirror, where she confronts a woman who "lived under the earth somewhere, or inside something, a cave or a huge building; sometimes she was on a boat. She was enormously powerful, almost like a goddess, but it was an unhappy power" (224). Joan does not recognize this woman at first. Her second descent occurs when she is knocked overboard into Lake Ontario during her faked suicide, a comic version of the dive from the canoe made by the narrator of *Surfacing*. In *The Divine Comedy*, Dante visits hell on his way to a vision of his true love, Beatrice, in paradise. Joan visits the more ambiguous territory of limbo, and instead of ascending to paradise, returns to earth. Her final descent is into the maze, often seen as an archetype, a primordial symbol, of the self. In one classical myth, Theseus meets the monstrous Minotaur at the centre of a maze and kills it. Atwood has remarked that "in gothic tales the maze is just a scare device. You have an old mansion with winding passages and a monster at the centre. . . . But the maze I use is a descent into the underworld" ("Interview" [Sandler] 16). This descent is found in worldwide mythology, including classical and Christian myths, where the descent into the underworld includes a confrontation with evil in preparation for rebirth. In psychological terms, it is a descent into the unconscious, where one comes to terms with one's deepest fears and frees oneself from one's mental chains (see Davey 164). For Joan, the struggle takes place not only in her imagination, but also in the text of the novel she is writing.

Literary Self-Creation and Recognition

Joan once again proves able to survive, this time by becoming not her own mother, but her own therapist. Her Gothic romances have been a way of maintaining her sanity, or at least the status quo, for a long time:

As long as I could spend a certain amount of time each week as Louisa, I was all right, I was patient and forbearing, warm, a sympathetic listener. But if I was cut off, if I couldn't work at my current Costume Gothic, I would become mean and irritable, drink too much and start to cry. (215)

The romances provide her with enough recognition, if only from her publishers, to survive, and with enough vicarious romance to make her lukewarm existence with Arthur tolerable. In Terremoto, however, the Gothic form begins to fall apart on Joan. This marks the beginning of the last days in the underworld of Terremoto, where Joan finally confronts her personal Minotaur: her relationship with her mother and her problematic attitude to men.

Joan and Her Mother

Her writing has failed her before:

For a while after my mother's death I couldn't write. The old plots no longer interested me, and a new one wouldn't do. I did try — I started a novel called *Storm over Castleford* — but the hero played billiards all the time and the heroine sat on the edge of her bed, alone at night, doing nothing. That was probably the closest to social realism I ever came. (182)

What has happened is that she has started to think about her mother as a person like herself, rather than as a "monster" (64), a person who must have had a dream of a good life, but had been stranded "in this house, this plastic-shrouded tomb from which there was no exit" (180). Joan starts to feel that she has been as unfair to her mother as life itself has been, and begins to want to know her mother better: "For the first time in my life I began to feel it was unfair that everyone had liked Aunt Lou but no one had liked my mother, not really" (181). These insights threaten what has been the source of her recurrent need to try to please her monster mother by succeeding in becoming the perfect heroine, if only in fantasy.

Joan's mother is clearly the unhappy goddess of the underworld. Joan only realizes this near the end of her stay in Terremoto:

It had been she standing behind me in the mirror, she was the one who was waiting around each turn, her voice whispered the words. She had been the lady in the boat, the death barge, the tragic lady with flowing hair and stricken eyes, the lady in the tower. She couldn't stand the view from her window, life was her curse. How could I renounce her? (331)

By blaming her mother for everything, Joan has turned her into a monster, and in the process of her rebellion, has turned herself into one too — first a physical grotesque, and then a psychological one. At the mythic level, Joan's mother is Hecate, the goddess of the underworld. As Atwood explains in *Survival*, she "presides over death and has oracular powers"; although she is "the Crone," "the most forbidding of the three" parts of "the Triple Goddess" (the others are "the elusive Diana or Maiden figure" and "the Venus figure, goddess of love"), she "is only one phase of a cycle; she is not sinister when viewed as part of a process. . . . But Hecate does become sinister when she is seen as the only alternative, as the whole of the range of possibilities for being female" (199). (Some critics have suggested that Joan's mother's three heads are those of Cerberus, the hound that guards the entrance to the underworld in the *Æneid*. It seems more plausible that these are the heads of the Triple Goddess.) Here, again, the issue of limited possibilities is raised. Joan can see her mother in only one static way.

Joan tries to escape her mother by leaving home, but "All this time I carried my mother around my neck like a rotting albatross. I dreamed about her often, my three-headed mother, menacing and cold" (215). The rotting albatross is an allusion to Samuel Taylor Coleridge's *The Rime of the Ancient Mariner*. The mariner kills an albatross, which brings a curse on his ship. As punishment, he must wear the dead bird around his neck; finally, he blesses some sea snakes, which lifts the curse. The psychological truth in this story, as Coleridge put it in another poem, is that "we receive but what we give" (375). By turning her mother into the dead monster mother, Joan has brought down a similar curse on herself. She, like the mariner's ship, seems to float, becalmed in a world filled with activity in which she plays no role. That Joan has "killed" her mother, who nonetheless still cares for her at some level, is indicated in her mother's appearance before her death at a séance. The medium, Leda Sprott comments, "I'm happy for you. . . . I had the feeling she's been trying to contact you for some time. She must be very concerned about you" (110).

Several critics, notably Barbara Godard, have connected the myth of Demeter and Persephone with the novel. In the best-known version of the myth, Hades, the god of the underworld, abducts Persephone, the daughter of Demeter the goddess of fertility. Demeter mourns ceaselessly for her lost child, and all life withers and dies. Finally, at the command of Zeus, Persephone is allowed to spend half of each year with her mother. Spring marks her return. In modern mother-daughter relationships, however, at least until recently, the mother has been taught to value in her daughter only that which is seen as valuable by men: beauty and docility. To ready the child for marriage is all that matters. Instead of mourning the loss of her child to a figure who represents death, the mother sees marriage as proof of her success. When Joan rejects her mother's vision, by turning herself into a monster no one will want to marry, with a "sasquatch-like . . . tread" (69), her mother rejects her. As Godard notes, the "mothers see their creations as monsters and reject them. . . . In turn, the daughters, in revolt, perceive their mothers as monsters" (36). A vicious circle of hostility replaces the fruitful cycle that symbolized the harmonious relationship of the goddess and her daughter. However, it is a circle: Joan does identify with her mother, although she certainly would vehemently deny it. As revealed by Joan's description of the images from the mirror sessions, her mother is not only Hecate, but also Persephone, the unhappy goddess of the underworld, imprisoned in a "plastic-shrouded tomb" (48), Rapunzel "with flowing hair" (331) and the Lady of Shalott "who couldn't stand the view from her window" (331), trapped in the sterile suburban "home" that has replaced the tower for middle-class women, waiting for a rescuer who never comes. In a sense, Joan has to rescue her mother before she can rescue herself, and this rescue entails giving up the idea that rescuers are invariably men. Once Joan starts recognizing that she and her mother's marriages are similarly unfulfilling, she will be able to comprehend that her mother is no more "monstrous" than Joan's adolescent "sasquatch" self.

Near the beginning of the novel, Joan imagines everyone from her past walking, like characters in a Fellini film, along a beach. Aunt Lou is the only one who is not looking at Joan. Then Joan realizes that the others are not looking at her, but waving at each other. They seem, like her, to be trapped in the need to have their identity confirmed by others, while Lou goes her own way: " 'That's just the way I am,' Aunt Lou said once. 'If other people can't handle it, that's their problem' " (86; I thank Lori Burwash, one of my students, for this insight). She loves Joan as a fat, snivelling child and never suggests Joan should change to please her (at least not until her will is read). Aunt Lou is not two-faced, nor does she require others to play a role for her. Although Barbara Rigney sees her as a negative figure because she introduces Joan to movies that stereotype women (72–73), other critics (Bromberg 22; Thomas 166; Johnston 17; Carrington 73) see her as, at least partly, a positive influence. Aunt Lou is far more motherly than Joan's real mother. She had an unhappy marriage, and was totally unprepared for domesticity, but finds a much more balanced life than Joan's mother does, raising her brother (Joan's father) and then helping his daughter. She works and loves without apology, however peculiar her job and her lover may seem. Joan has inherited her resourcefulness, as Aunt Lou is "all for dismissing handicaps or treating them as obstacles to be overcome" (82). Joan's roles as "kindly aunt and wisewoman" (91), and her "wonderful personality" (119), are based on Lou's example. Aunt Lou is a writer who writes solely for women, about matters both sexual and romantic. Her photograph featured on a booklet called *You're Growing Up*, Lou is, to Joan, "like a movie star, sort of" (83). No wonder Joan chooses Lou's name as a pen name. Her legacy allows Joan to undo at least some of the harmful results of her rebellion against her mother and begin an independent life: to grow up.

Society's Construction of Identity

Because of her father's abdication of his role, and Joan's resistance to her mother's attempt to mould her, Joan is perhaps even more susceptible than most to wider cultural influences. Most teenagers get many of their ideas about how life ought to be from their peers and the media; for Joan, these are primary influences.

The first page of *Lady Oracle* mentions that Joan wants her death to be "neat and simple" like "the basic black dress with a single strand of pearls much praised by fashion magazines when I was fifteen." Then she comments on "visions," obviously derived from advertising, of herself "as a Mediterranean splendor, golden-brown, striding with laughing teeth into an aqua sea, carefree at last" (3). Next she mentions a fantasy obviously derived from Gothic romance, and Fellini and Disney movies. Since childhood, Joan has voraciously soaked up fantasies from magazines, movies, ballet, her mother's historical romances, her father's murder mysteries, opera, fairy tales, and, not least, her aunt's advice columns. All these convey an idea of how society ought to be and how women ought to behave in it.

Arthur, Joan thinks, would view the extreme gender moulding undergone even by the inappropriately fat child as simply wrong:

> What a shame, he'd say, how destructive to me were the attitudes of society, forcing me into a mold of femininity that I could never fit, stuffing me into those ridiculous pink tights, those spangles, those outmoded, cramping ballet slippers. How much better for me if I'd been accepted for what I was and had learned to accept myself, too. Very true, very right, very pious. But it's still not so simple. I wanted those things, that fluffy skirt, that glittering tiara. I liked them. (102)

The problem is that the child wants to conform to the values of its peers, and that culture not only moulds us, it makes us love the mould. And, after all, Arthur's puritanical repudiation of any cultural frill is far less attractive than Joan's cheerful acceptance of all its most gaudy and vulgar manifestations.

Further, simply to reject all evidence of the feminine is not the answer: this rejection leads to the obliteration of anything but the masculine, rather than to the undoing of gender stereotypes. Consider, after all, the fate of the two other "fat girls" at Joan's school. Monica is accepted by the boys, "but as another boy," because she wears leather, smokes, and swears. The shy Theresa, dressed like a matron, had "the traditional fat-girl reputation" as a slut (92). If these are the alternatives (and they usually are), to be crammed into spangles does not seem so oppressive after all. Joan, by wanting the apparently impossible, shows how arbitrary the social conception of what is possible for a woman really is. She wants to be the Fat Lady and a ballet dancer. She wants to succeed as a fat ballet dancer, a fat tightrope walker, a fat figure skater. These fantasies are only outrageous because of the strictures of society, and part of us is tempted to side with Joan. Why shouldn't she, like Chairman Mao, be fat and successful too? She doesn't want to be forced into a choice, she wants to get out of the confines of the stereotypes. She constantly comes up against society's refusal to allow women to do anything reminiscent of the feminine *and* claim a place in the masculine realm. For example, Arthur's roommates quickly teach her that "One could not, apparently, be both a respected female savant and a scullery maid" (170). But just as Joan once put everything within reach into her mouth, she tries now, at least at the level of fantasy, to have it all.

Ballerinas, Butterflies, and Fat Ladies

Not surprisingly, Joan's experience in Miss Flegg's ballet class marks her for life. Joan "idealized ballet dancers" because "it was something girls could *do*" (39; emphasis added), although her mother is clearly more interested in it because she hopes it will improve the way Joan looks. Joan's noisy, enthusiastic, and even destructive practice sessions contrast with the girls at the dress rehearsal who "finished and costumed . . . were standing against the wall so as not to damage themselves, inert as temple sacrifices" (43). Ballet, although it requires a good deal of muscle and prowess, is designed to disguise the effort, and the main reason these girls are enrolled is to make them graceful and appealing to watch, to ready them for the gaze of the hero. Joan, however, has missed this point and still believes in merit over appearance: since she knows the steps she cannot understand her rejection. Forced to abandon her butterfly costume and dance the role of a mothball, she must therefore, against her will, scatter the illusion (as a mothball scatters butterflies) she longs to take part in. The romance turns into farce, as it so often will for Joan:

I threw myself into the part, it was a dance of rage and destruction, tears rolled down my cheeks behind the fur, the butterflies would die; my feet hurt for days afterwards. "This isn't me," I kept saying to myself, "they're making me do it"; yet even though I was concealed in the teddy-bear suit, which flopped about me and made me sweat, I felt naked and exposed, as if this ridiculous dance was the truth about me and everyone could see it. (47)

Her anger here is aimed at her mother and Miss Flegg, who have first hooked her on the romantic illusion and then declared her unworthy of it ("who would think of marrying a mothball" [48]). She will never be able to have the correctly passive relationship to romance again. However much she tries to hide it, she has learned the power and rewards of creativity. She writes romances instead of simply consuming them. Seduced by the count, she turns around and seduces Arthur. But she denies her anger and the power it gives her: "This isn't me . . . they're making me do it." But the anger is hers, and the dance wins the praise of the audience, who yell "Bravo mothball!" because, instead of the rote flittings of the others, her part is original: "There were no steps to my dance, as I hadn't been taught any, so I made it up as I went along" (47).

Her response to her own story is similarly original. The rigid patterning of the Gothic romance works, like ballet, to conform women to the requirements of gender stereotyping, and differs greatly from the complicated story that we are reading here, told by Joan to the reporter, which upsets and parodies the illusions of romance. Joan has always believed in the narrow view of conventional styles and patterns, but by the end of the novel, things have started to go seriously wrong with her imagination's ability to produce Gothic plots: "Sympathy for Felicia was out of the question, it was against the rules, it would foul up the plot completely. . . . [But] I was getting tired of Charlotte, with her intact virtue and her tidy ways. Wearing her was like wearing a hair shirt, she made me itchy . . ." (321). Her last line in the novel, where she notes that she will never be "a very tidy person" (345), holds out hope that she will stop trying to cram herself into inappropriate conventional roles, and instead accept the odd, and even floppy costume that will allow her the artistic freedom to express her feelings.

Joan's favourite fantasy costume has butterfly wings. Butterflies have long been symbols of new life, and even of the life to come, and for Joan, the idea of magical transformations is always appealing. But butterflies are not necessarily positive symbols, as Joan comes to realize: "So what if you turn into a butterfly? Butterflies die too" (114). Caterpillars, like the foetus that symbolizes Joan's relation to existence, have hidden potential. Like the child Joan, at least in the eyes of her mother, caterpillars are destructive and spend all their time eating and crawling. Butterflies are beautiful and spend their time flitting: they are fragile and die easily. From Joan's perspective, the problem with butterflies may well be that they are finished, clearly defined, perfected. She remains a hungry caterpillar on her own terms, rather than turn into her mother's perfected butterfly. Joan is, as she says, hooked on plots, events, transformations, change: caterpillars undergo metamorphoses, but butterflies just die.

Metamorphoses, Rebirths, and Magical Transformations

The novel is full of transformations, some more magical than others. Joan becomes a blimp, and then subsides. The Royal Porcupine becomes Chuck. Various men turn into princes, briefly, and then turn into villains. Joan's father's job is to bring people back from the dead: "You'd be surprised how many of them are glad. That they've been able to . . . come back, have another chance" (70). He himself has been transformed by history from a killer into a rescuer; as an anaesthetist, he "kills" people to save them; his daily life is a process of threat and rescue.

Joan's mother, like Joan, believes in magical transformations, as her redecorating habits reveal:

It was a new house and she had just finished getting it into shape; now that it was finally right she didn't want anything touched, she wanted it static and dustless and final, until that moment when she would see what a mistake she had made and the painters or movers would arrive once more, trailing disruption. (68)

Her "living rooms . . . look[ed] like museum displays or more accurately like the show windows of Eaton's and Simpson's" (68). Museums always have connotations of death and the underworld for

Atwood. Interestingly, Arthur's behaviour is similar to that of Joan's mother. His infatuation with a new cause is like his mother-in-law's with a new style: "In quick succession he went through Vietnam and sheltering draft dodgers, student revolt, and an infatuation with Mao" (212). Neither of them breaks through the pattern of infatuation and disillusionment that matches Joan's with her Gothic heroes and villains. The psychological dead ends reveal that none of them can undertake the most difficult transformation of all: of themselves. Instead, they try to change the world and other people to fit their fantasies, refusing to learn anything at all from their failures.

THE GOTHIC THEME

Canada as Gothic Heroine

Significantly, the Gothic has been seen as a Canadian genre (Northey, Mandel) because of the constant search of those involved in Canadian culture for a distinctively Canadian identity. Caught between two powerful parents, Great Britain and the United States, the Canadian hero/ine typically has trouble distinguishing himself or herself from the two. Worse, despite a nominal independence, true cultural or economic separation seems impossible. In *Survival*, Atwood states that the realization that Canada is a cultural and economic colony of the United States underlies the central theme of Canadian literature. The Canadian colonial outlook gives rise to certain distinctive "victim positions," which "are the same whether you are a victimized country, a victimized minority group or a victimized individual" (36). Canada's obsession with the United States resembles the Gothic heroine's obsession with the hero who is sometimes seen as threat and sometimes as a rescuer. Joan takes a victim position by refusing to grow up and play an adult role; she prefers to blame her mother or the nearest male villain for her problems.

The Gothic Romance

Joan herself outlines the typical features of a Gothic romance: "There were the sufferings, the hero in the mask of a villain, the villain in the mask of a hero, the flights, the looming death, the sense of being imprisoned . . ." followed by true love and a happy ending (234). For Joan, the Gothic world is heaven:

> I longed for the simplicity of that world, where happiness was possible and wounds were only ritual ones. Why had I been closed out from that impossible white paradise where love was as final as death, and banished to this other place [the real world] where everything changed and shifted? (286)

Trapped as she is inside her own family, deeply desiring to see her parents as good and kind, even though they appear indifferent or even actively malevolent, the simplistic morality of the genre appeals to her.

The readership for historical romances and Gothic novels of the sort Joan begins to write has generally consisted of women. Why do women find these novels so appealing? Recent studies of popular culture have argued that women find them appealing because these novels first arouse fears common to most women, and then proceed to calm them. Always on the verge of ruin, the traditional Gothic heroine ends up married to a rich and handsome aristocrat, often the same man who seemed to threaten her at the novel's beginning. Or, already married, she goes through a period of terrible fear that her husband is really a villain, to find, in the end, that he is the hero he was always supposed to be. But what is the nature of the looming threat epitomized in the title of Joan's last Gothic, *Stalked by Love*?

The Fear of Men in Reality and Romance

The primary threat at the heart of the Gothic romance is the threat of male violence. The terror at the heart of *Lady Oracle*, the threat that drives Joan to a fake suicide, is apparently posed, however, by several fairly harmless men. Joan seems to be overreacting when she suspects one or all of them of harassing her with heavy breathing over the phone, dead animals on the doorstep, and threatening notes. Finally she comes to the rather unconvincing conclusion that Arthur is responsible, just as she earlier came to the rather unconvincing conclusion that her equally mildmannered father was responsible for her mother's murder.

Atwood has to make these men fairly innocuous, because if she had made any of them true Gothic villains, the obvious solution to Joan's problems would have been simply to find a Gothic hero. But, as Joan discovers, all men are complex mixtures of both, which complicates life enormously. As a child, she wonders about the man who exposed himself to her, gave her daffodils, and perhaps later untied her from the bridge: "Was the man who untied me a rescuer or a villain? Or, an even more baffling thought: was it possible for a man to be both at once?" (61). The answer to this last question is "yes," although Joan rarely realizes it.

Atwood is also making it clear that although these men seem, as individuals, quite harmless, they nonetheless do represent a threat to Joan because they live in a society that gives more power to men than women. Thus they come to represent the closing down of possibility. And this closing down is not simply the result of the heroine's having made a poor choice. That Arthur is so harmless makes the point clear. He is hardly a monster of lust: Joan seduces him. In their first encounter, he is distributing ban-the-bomb pamphlets; it is she who, lost in a Gothic plot that causes her to see him as an attacker, scratches him. Yet neither his sexual naïvety nor his political sophistication makes him sensitive to Joan's needs. He proposes to her partly for financial reasons: Joan "would keep [her] job, of course; that way he wouldn't have to accept so much money from his parents" (198). Even the socialist Arthur takes it for granted that she will put him through university, not to mention hold the rabbit ears when they watch their antiquated television. His casual assumption of superiority and Joan's acquiescence derive not from their personal characteristics (he is hardly the domineering, macho type, nor she the swooning virgin), but from their upbringing in a system that has trained them both to take inequality between the sexes for granted. Although it might be possible for a reader to decide that the solution to Marian's problem with Peter in *The Edible Woman* is for her to find a more sensitive man (the androgynous Duncan, perhaps), it is clearly not just another man that Joan needs. From the boy kneeling in the puddle in Braeside, through Zerdo, Paul the Polish count, and the Royal Porcupine, all have assumed that she will conform to their desires, and all express absolutely no interest in finding out about hers. Zerdo wants a mother for his children and an efficient cashier for his restaurant. Paul wants a compliant mistress. The Royal Porcupine wants, first, to compete

57

with her as an artist, and then to take her over from Arthur, as his sudden personality change indicates.

Joan doesn't need a new man, she needs a society that provides her with a fairer deal and women generally with a better future, which may explain why she decides to write science fiction at the end of the novel. Barring that, she needs to change her own feeling that she isn't worth more attention than Arthur can give her (he fails to notice either her secret novel writing or her affair with the Royal Porcupine).

In showing Joan as apparently overreacting to the male threat, Atwood could be accused of conforming to the stereotypical belief that women fail to use their reason, preferring to operate on highly inaccurate intuitions and highly suspect interpretations. And, perhaps not surprisingly, the novel has been read this way. Wilfred Cude concludes that just as Joan doesn't "have the least idea" (132) who is harassing her heroine, Charlotte (*Lady Oracle* 132), so Atwood "might have taken a leaf from her character's book, that she too doesn't have the least idea who was harassing her heroine" (Cude, "Nobody" 35). He argues that Atwood must mean something by this failure to tie up a loose end, and concludes:

> The lesson we learn by following out this one loose end in the novel is that Joan will have her mysteries whatever happens, she will capitalize on the bizarre if it occurs or dream up the bizarre if it does not, careening headlong through her insane course with no concern for who else gets hurt. (36)

He concludes that the real mystery in the novel is that of Joan's mother's death, and that in trying to imagine her father as the murderer, Joan is simply shielding herself from her own guilt in abandoning her mother emotionally, and thus contributing to the alcoholism that probably explains her fatal fall. Cude, then, does read Joan not only as an airhead, but also as an emotional monster, whose overheated imagination serves to hide her irresponsibility. This interpretation matches that of feminists, to a degree. As Tania Modleski notes:

> we can see how Gothics, like Harlequins, perform the function of giving expression to women's hostility towards men while simultaneously allowing them to repudiate it. Because the male appears to be the outrageous persecutor, the reader can allow

herself a measure of anger against him; yet at the same time she can identify with a heroine who is entirely without malice and innocent of any wrongdoing. (66)

Nonetheless, good reasons for Joan's apparent overreaction can be found: she doesn't just invent the threat. Atwood makes it impossible to dismiss Joan as merely overimaginative or even slightly crazy. As Beryl Langer puts it, she "knows that she is the object of some man's violent fantasy, the intended prey of an anonymous hunter" (93); her assumption that this man is someone she knows makes the situation seem less alarming than if it were someone she doesn't, and, therefore, her desperate attempts to claim it is someone she knows make sense. Cude, like Joan herself in interpreting her mother, sees only how adults who view themselves as victims harm others. He fails to see how victims have themselves been constructed through suffering.

After all, Joan has been threatened. Someone really is harassing her, sending her death threats. Paul really has a gun; Chuck really does suggest jumping off the Toronto-Dominion Centre with her in his arms. The "bad man" really does expose himself to her in the park, and may even have found her helpless, tied to a bridge. Cude, like Joan's mother, acts as if Joan "had planted the bushes in the ravine and concealed the bad men behind them" (50). Both prefer to blame the victim rather than examine the system that creates victims.

Although the most serious threat posed implicitly or explicitly in the Gothic is violent rape or murder, another threat is that of male indifference. Since male love is the only way a woman can be socially validated, some romances even put forward the message that to be raped is better than to be ignored. Not surprisingly, these romances are unpopular with many women readers (Radway 165).

Feminist critics have argued that Gothic novels appeal to women because they at first echo the fears their readers have of violence or indifference from men, and then allay them by showing how the violence or indifference originates in love, and has been misinterpreted by the overfearful woman. As Janice Radway concludes, "The romantic narrative demonstrates that a woman must learn to trust her man and to believe that he loves her deeply even in the face of massive evidence to the contrary" (149). Radway also maintains that

In suggesting that the cruelty and indifference that the hero exhibits toward the heroine in the early part of the novel are really of no consequence because they *actually* originated in love and affection, the romance effectively asserts that there are other signs for these two emotions than the traditional ones of physical caresses, oral professions of commitment, and thoughtful care. (151)

Or as Joan puts it about Arthur:

Heroes were supposed to be aloof. His indifference was feigned, I told myself. Any moment now his hidden depths would heave to the surface; he would be passionate and confess his long-standing devotion. I would then confess mine, and we would be happy. (Later I decided that his indifference at that time was probably not feigned at all. . . .) (197)

Arthur stays aloof, and Joan, for a long time, pretends she prefers it that way.

Women read Gothic novels because they have real fears and need reassurance, something that the novels give them, although the indifference or violence that inspire the fears remains unchanged. Romances, in a sense, train women to interpret male behaviour as loving even when it patently is not. Statistics make clear that in Canada many women are beaten, raped, or killed by men, and that these men are more likely to be husbands, partners, friends, or acquaintances than strangers. Reading romances does nothing to help women faced with real violence; in fact, this reading may serve to keep women in violent relationships and make them vulnerable to attacks by men. Nor does it incline women to require more warmth and emotional commitment from men, because "heroes [are] supposed to be aloof" (*Lady* 197).

Joan's Complicity

Joan knows full well that in writing romances she is engaged in a dubious enterprise:

These books, with their covers featuring gloomy, foreboding castles and apprehensive maidens in modified nightgowns, hair streaming in the wind, eyes bulging like those of a goiter victim, toes poised for flight, would be considered trash of the lowest order. Worse than trash, for didn't they exploit the masses, corrupt by distracting, and perpetuate degrading stereotypes of women as helpless and persecuted? They did and I knew it, but I couldn't stop. (30)

Because of her victim mentality, she feels she can't stop, and thus ends up rationalizing what she is up to. She sees herself as helping her readers:

Life had been hard on them and they had not fought back, they'd collapsed like soufflés in a high wind. Escape wasn't a luxury for them, it was a necessity. . . . And when they were too tired to invent escapes of their own, mine were available for them at the corner drugstore, neatly packaged like the other painkillers. (30–31)

Just as drugs only dull the pain for a while, and may eventually lead to disastrous addiction, so Joan's romances do not provide a solution to her readers' problems, but only serve to mask them.

Leda Sprott warns Joan about misusing her talent for writing, but Joan doesn't pay attention:

You have great powers, I told you that before, but you've been afraid to develop them. . . . You do not choose a gift, it chooses you, and if you deny it it will make use of you in any case, though perhaps in a less desirable way. . . . When I had no truth to tell, I told them what they wanted to hear. I shouldn't have done that. You may think it's harmless, but it isn't. (207)

Certainly, it seems entirely possible that Joan's Gothics do her even more harm than they do her readers.

Loss of Identity in the Gothic Romance

The primary terror at the heart of the female Gothic tradition is the terror of male rejection or violence. But there is more. Another part of the terror is that of the loss of identity, a loss that can lead to madness. Some of this terror appears to come from the situation typical of nineteenth-century middle-class women on the verge of marriage, the group that originally formed the main readership for the Gothic genre. Young, innocent, ignorant, and protected, a woman of this group had to move away from her family where her identity, however restricted, was secure, and into a new relationship with a relative stranger, a stranger with sexual rights and absolute authority. A woman who had barely dealt with her relationship with her mother was then faced with the prospect of becoming one. How did she separate herself from her own mother, her own children? The question "Where does the self end and the other begin?" is the source of much of the terror in the Gothic.

Names, generally a sign of an individual identity, fail Joan in her quest. She has been named after someone, Joan Crawford, whose real name is something else: Lucille LeSueur. Later she wonders if she had been named after Saint Joan, first a victor, then a martyr-victim. When she herself picks a pseudonym, it is her aunt's name. Neither her own name nor her aunt's provide her with a distinctive identity, and, of course, taking Arthur's name doesn't either.

Furthermore, she finds that she is not reflected by others, that they do not see her, either because she is fat and not worth looking at, or because she has become thin and unrecognizable. For example, she recognizes Marlene, but Marlene doesn't remember her. In one way, she hopes that her former tormenter will not remember her as a fat, blubbering Brownie, but neither is it reassuring that Marlene has forgotten her. It may mean that Joan is invisible, not really there.

For Joan, the terror connected to the loss of identity is also found in mirrors, where we normally expect to see our reflection. Joan loses herself in a nightmare mirror that seems to lead to the underworld, or stares at her odd reflection in the funhouse mirrors at the Canadian National Exhibition. The terror of loss of identity is also connected with uncontrollable doubling or reduplication as caused by a triple mirror like the one that Joan's mother uses to apply makeup, or that Joan uses to produce her automatic writing. Doubling also occurs in the distorted reflections of the media:

> it was as if someone with my name were out there in the real world, impersonating me, saying things I'd never said but which appeared in the newspapers, doing things for which I had to take the consequences: my dark twin, my funhouse-mirror reflection. . . . She wanted to kill me and take my place. (252)

Joan fears being taken over by her public persona, a legitimate fear for someone whose sense of self is insecure. Joan also begins to feel double when she looks in a mirror and sees her fat outline around her thin body (216), and when her fantasies of the Fat Lady or Felicia start taking over. The notion of doubling is also connected with monsters and monstrous births; to put it in schoolyard form, if Joan's mother is a monster, what does that make her?

Atwood says that in *Surfacing*, "the ghost that one sees is in fact a fragment of one's own self which has split off . . ." ("Margaret" [Gibson] 29). According to many psychologists, what frightens us most is our own destructive and dark impulses, which we escape and deny by projecting onto others. Joan is so angry at her mother that she cannot express it, or even admit it. In order to protect herself, then, she has to transform her mother into a monster who deserves such hatred and anger. So Joan projects her own monstrous impulses onto her mother, and later onto her various lovers. In order to have relationships with others that are not simply relationships with projections of ourselves, we have to learn to come to terms with our own dark side. Joan's failure to do so explains her feeling that

> Love was merely a tool, smiles were another tool, they were both just tools for accomplishing certain ends. . . . I felt I'd never really loved anyone, not Paul, not Chuck the Royal Porcupine, not even Arthur. I'd polished them with my love and expected them to shine, brightly enough to return my own reflection, enhanced and sparkling. (284–85)

Love as she has experienced it is simply a kind of narcissism, or, worse even than self-love, a desperate struggle to please in order that the other will reflect a positive version of the self rather than turn away in indifference or disgust.

Historical Gothic Romances

The Gothic novel has a long history, dating from the late eighteenth century. Significantly, Atwood's area of specialization as a graduate student at Harvard University included the Gothic. Although thousands of Gothic romances have been written, a few are of particular significance. Mrs. Radcliffe's *The Mysteries of Udolpho* (1794), is often seen as a model of the genre. (Atwood's setting her Gothic partly in Italy may be a kind of homage to Radcliffe's fondness for Italian settings.) Two novels that are less conventionally Gothic, although still strongly related to the genre, are Charlotte Brontë's *Jane Eyre* (1847), and Emily Brontë's *Wuthering Heights* (1847). Perhaps even more closely related to *Lady Oracle*, because it too is a parody of a Gothic novel rather than a real one, is Jane Austen's *Northanger Abbey* (1818); a comparison of the two is instructive.

In *Northanger Abbey*, Catherine Morland, on a visit to the home of Henry Tilney, the man she is falling in love with, convinces herself that Henry's father, General Tilney, murdered his wife. Henry guesses what she is thinking, and is profoundly shocked. Catherine, reproved, is horribly ashamed:

> The visions of romance were over. Catherine was completely awakened. Henry's address, short as it had been, had more thoroughly opened her eyes to the extravagance of her late fancies than all their several disappointments had done. Most grievously was she humbled. Most bitterly did she cry. (201)

However, Catherine shortly discovers that although General Tilney is not a wife murderer as she had suspected, he is a tyrannical materialist. His materialism and insensitivity make his children unhappy, and must have made his wife's life a misery.

The dark fate awaiting the middle-class woman may not be violence, rape, or murder (although these, as statistics make clear, are entirely possible), but the sterile and unfulfilled life that may well have driven Joan's mother to alcohol and suicide. Joan's father refuses both his wife and his daughter more than the most token gestures of emotional support, or the slightest hint that either of them might be necessary to him either economically or emotionally. Instead, he escapes to the powerful world of the hospital; Arthur's emotional life is in the university and his political work. Both Joan and her mother, however, spend a good deal of time trying to involve themselves in their husbands' lives, only to discover that they are far less important to their husbands than their husbands are to them.

Like Catherine in *Northanger Abbey*, Joan is presented as someone who foolishly takes Gothic romances too seriously and who must learn to think for herself, to trust her own judgement, rather than to write everything around her into a Gothic plot. But both novels reveal that it is not enough simply to discard fantasies derived from literature as false; this is to neglect the understanding that comes through the emotions that drive the Gothic novel. Catherine is correct to feel that the general is not trustworthy; Joan is correct when she senses that her mother and Arthur do not love her very well. Somehow, the complex connections between fantasy, art, and the real world must be carefully worked out. Neither Catherine nor Joan are well served by their wholesale attempts to see life through the simplistic structures of the Gothic plot. But at least they are using their imaginations to interpret the world; if they add their reason to their imaginations they will, both Austen and Atwood imply, be far better able to confront life's complexities. Atwood's own decision to become a novelist rather than an academic critic may have resulted from her belief that reason and imagination, logic and emotion, must work together.

Gothic Thinking

Margaret Atwood explained to J.R. (Tim) Struthers that *Lady Oracle* is an "anti-gothic," and continued:

> I think in an anti-gothic what you're doing is examining the perils of gothic thinking, as it were. And one of the perils of gothic thinking is that gothic thinking means that you have a scenario in your head which involves certain roles — the dark, experienced man, who is possibly evil and possibly good, the rescuer, the mad wife, and so on — and that as you go to real life you tend to cast real people in these roles as Joan does. Then when you find out that the real people don't fit these two-dimensional roles, you can either discard the roles and try to deal with the real person or discard the real person. ("Interview" 23–24)

Joan's Gothic plots simply kill off anyone who is in the way of a satisfactorily romantic outcome: Felicia "had to die. In my books all wives were eventually either mad or dead, or both" (321). Likewise, she murders her fat self. Similarly, the Royal Porcupine kills off his romantic lover self in order to transform himself into what he thinks is a suitable husband figure. Both Joan and the Royal Porcupine even extend this behaviour to real people, each other included. Joan has "murdered" her mother, who then haunts her. Joan and the Porcupine don't realize that their fantasies and their roles cannot simply be killed off at will. When Joan finds she has to let Felicia live at the end of *Stalked by Love*, it seems clear that Joan is starting to find Gothic thinking unsatisfactory. Like Joan, Felicia is redheaded, passionate, messy, and (at least in one version) fat. Killing her off is a form of self-loathing, as Joan has begun to realize.

Gothic thinking appears to extend further than women's thinking about men. It is a term that can be fruitfully applied to extremist thinking of any kind. Arthur sees the world in terms even more black and white than Joan's:

> He never had fights with people, he never talked things out with them. He would simply decide, by some dark, complicated process of evaluation, that these people were unworthy. Not that they'd done something unworthy, but that unworthiness was innate in them. Once he'd made his judgment, that was it. No trial, no redress. (213–14)

As Cathy and Arnold Davidson point out, "the three male characters fantasize every bit as much as Joan does. They all strike poses, and when pose encounters pose, the necessary consequence is misunderstanding" (170–71). Paul's vision of the international Communist conspiracy, Arthur's various left-wing fantasies, the Royal Porcupine's anarchistic nihilism, are all male political fantasies that obscure these men's view of Joan as much as Joan's Gothic fantasies obscure her view of them.

Joan points out that her audience reads romance because such political fantasies don't appeal to them: "War, politics and explorations up the Amazon, those other great escapes, were by and large denied them, and they weren't much interested in hockey or football, games they couldn't play" (32). Women are not usually permitted to take part in the real-life effects of these fantasies, and prefer to stick to romance, their special territory. Despite her obedient reading of the works of Arthur's latest political hero, Joan sees the problems inherent in his Gothic thinking:

> I empathized with anything in pain. . . . For this reason, as Arthur pointed out more than once, my politics were sloppy. I

didn't like firing squads; I never felt that those toppled from power deserved what got done to them, no matter what they'd done in their turn. "Naïve humanism," Arthur called it. He liked it fine when it was applied to him, though. (90)

Male political fantasies that lead to physical pain, violence, and death seem more dangerous than female fantasies that lead to psychological pain, but just as gender roles are reciprocal, so are these fantasy worlds. If one is to be changed, the other one must be too.

When Linda Sandler asked Atwood, "what society comes closest to your idea of the good society?" she responded:

There isn't such a society. . . . I say jokingly that I'm a William Morrisite, but Morris is impossible. . . . Any attempt to implement Morris' utopia would impose a lot of things on a lot of people. . . . What do you do then? What do you do if somebody doesn't buy your ideal society? You end up shooting people. What kind of ideal is that? ("Interview" 27)

Here Atwood points out the problems of extremist thinking at the political level, and for her, of course, the public world of power politics extends right into the private world of romance. Fantasies interact with reality at all levels of society; not just in the lives of those marginal figures — women, children, and artists — but also in the lives of the powerful. However, because the powerful can implement their fantasies more successfully, these fantasies are often glorified as truth, reality, the way things are, the real world.

Stalked by Love *and* Lady Oracle *as Gothic*

Their ambiguous endings alone disqualify Joan's *Stalked by Love* and Atwood's *Lady Oracle* from fitting into the category of romance, although both have many Gothic elements. The plot of *Lady Oracle* does resemble that of a typical, popular female Gothic in some respects. A Gothic plot essentially tells of a woman whose social identity has been disrupted, usually by removal from a familiar environment to an unfamiliar one. Her encounter with the hero at first leads to misunderstanding, as she believes he is only interested in her sexually. Vulnerable to him sexually, and often economically and legally dependent as well, the woman becomes fearful. Finally, by an act of tenderness, he overcomes the misunderstanding. Her recovery of identity comes when she gains his love. However, Joan herself is responsible for her loss of identity. She is the one who decides to abandon her past, time after time. She is the one who removes herself from one situation to the next. And there are several heroes, rather than one. Nor is she always worried about their sexual interest: she is glad, for example, that Paul is interested in her sexually (151). Her behaviour reveals that she is not the helpless victim that the romance heroine, however plucky, must be. Clearly, although she identifies strongly with these victims, she in fact has far more control over what happens to her than she would like to admit, something conveyed metaphorically by the fact that she not only reads Gothic romances, but also writes them. In fact, several critics, notably Clara Thomas and Lucy Freibert, have noticed that Atwood has mixed several genres in the novel, particularly a comic parody of the popular Gothic and the picaresque, but also the Bildungsroman (the novel of education) and the Künstlerroman (the novel about the development of an artist).

As Freibert explains in her article "The Artist as Picaro," the picaresque is a literary form where "a protagonist usually of uncertain origins" is "thrust into society early, and left totally dependent on the whims of Fortune," and "cast from one adventure to another" (23), like Moll Flanders or Tom Jones. *Lady Oracle*'s plot is picaresque in that the links between one episode and the next seem arbitrary. Joan's decisions are irrational and rushed, and even though there is always an explanation for them, it usually seems inadequate (see Rosengarten). But the point is that in each case she is acting on intuition and emotion alone, rather than invoking her intelligence as well. Because she has been brought up to regard her lovers as romantic heroes who love her passionately, whether they appear to or not, when they start to treat her badly or ignore her she can't simply confront herself or them with the fact and work it through. That would undermine her whole theory of male-female relations, and open her own behaviour to direct criticism, something that her insecurity cannot allow her to risk. Instead she escapes. The traditional picaro is a master of disguise and trickery and loves the excitement of danger, like Joan: "I was an artist, an escape artist. I'd sometimes talked about love and commitment, but the real romance of my life was that between Houdini and his ropes and locked trunk..." (335).

Although the traditional picaresque has some female heroines, it is usually seen as a parody of the heroic romance, where the hero's virtue and prowess win over evil. *Don Quixote*, for example, is such a parody, where the hero, like Joan, bases too much of his behaviour on a literary form and in his eagerness to emulate the heroes of old, ends up mistaking windmills for giants. By mixing genres, Atwood conveys in her own complex plot structure her message that life is too complicated to be tied to simplistic plot structures that are tied, in turn, to simplistic gender roles.

Stalked by Love, although its ending must be regarded as atypical or incomplete, is far closer to the conventions of the Gothic. Charlotte's mother's death has left her to her own resources in a dangerous world. Her first encounter with Redmond is typical in that he displays sexual interest that she finds oppressive:

> *She remembered the way his eyes had moved over her, appraising the curves of her firm young body, which were only partially concealed by her cheap, badly fitting black crepe dress. She had sufficient experience with the nobility to know how they looked upon women like herself, who through no fault of their own were forced to earn their own livings. . . . Already she had begun to hate him.* (26)

But romance readers know the hate won't last. Felicia, Redmond's imperious and unfaithful wife, is clearly set up for displacement. As Joan explains,

> Charlotte would then be free to become a wife in her turn. But first she would have a final battle with Redmond and hit him with something (a candelabrum, a poker, a stone, any hard sharp object would do), knocking him out and inducing brain fever with hallucinations, during which his features and desires would be purified by suffering and he would murmur her name. . . . That was one course of action. The other would be a final attempt on her life, with a rescue by Redmond, after which he

would reveal how deeply he loved her, with optional brain fever on her part. (317–18)

Felicia is on the decline, Charlotte on the ascendant, because, "in addition to Redmond she would get the emeralds, the family silver, deeds of land stowed away in attics, she would rearrange the furniture and give Felicia's clothes to the Crippled Civilians ... and generally throw her weight around" (318). Charlotte is looking forward to behaving just as Joan's mother had after Aunt Lou's death (118), and suddenly the power struggle between Charlotte and Felicia is starting to resemble Joan's messy power struggle with her tidy mother. In essence, Joan begins to realize that her heroines, tidy, virginal, and conventional, represent her mother's wish for her. To kill off Felicia, then, is to kill off, again, that part of herself that her mother (and most of society, in fact) deemed unacceptable, that is, the part that is loving, passionate, emotional, creative, and unconventional. When the plot stalls, Joan briefly considers turning to realism, but decides she can't forego "the feeling of release when everything turned out right. ... Redmond would kiss Charlotte so that her eyeballs rolled right back into her head, and then they could both vanish. When would they be joyful enough, when would my life be my own?" (321–22). Joan's constant conformity in her romances to the dictates not only of the genre, but also of society (women should define themselves by the love of a good man) and her internalized mother (she should be slender, tidy, and beautiful), helps her to deal with the misery that her mother's unhappiness brought her, but ultimately Joan realizes that it won't work: "My mother was a vortex, a dark vacuum, I would never be able to make her happy. Or anyone else. Maybe it was time for me to stop trying" (331). Joan has refused to conform in the past, and she is starting to refuse again. She is finally coming to realize that her life will only be her own when she stops compulsively trying to please not only her mother, but everybody else as well.

She needs, though, to finish her romance in order to get the money to escape the mysterious man Mr. Vitroni has warned her is inquiring after her in the village. Charlotte enters the maze: "*It was noon when Charlotte entered the maze. She took the precaution of fastening one end of a ball of knitting wool ... at the entrance; she did not intend to lose her way*" (333). Nonetheless, Joan loses her narrative thread at this point: "I'd taken a wrong turn somewhere; there was something, some fact or clue, that I had overlooked" (334). And here is where *Stalked by Love* begins to diverge from the conventions of the Gothic.

What even some astute critics have missed is that the next attempt at the maze is made by Felicia, who, like Joan, is a confident wife, rather than an imperilled virgin. That the confusion is intended by Atwood is clear, as the relevant passage simply begins: "*It was noon when she entered the maze.*" However, when this heroine finds herself in "*the central plot*" she discovers four women, two of whom "*looked a lot like her, with red hair and green eyes and small white teeth*" (341). These women are Joan, Felicia, the Fat Lady and Louisa K. Delacourt. But it is Felicia who is confronted with the exit, a door that resembles the door to Joan's flat, and it is Felicia who refuses to fall into Redmond's waiting arms. She realizes that if she goes through the door, he will kill her and replace her with another woman, "*thin and flawless*" like Charlotte (342). Thwarted, Redmond transforms himself into a series of men, the first with a surgeon's "*white gauze mask,*" the next with "*mauve-tinted spectacles, then a red beard and moustache,*" then the "*burning eyes and icicle teeth*" of the man in Joan's book of poetry, and finally Arthur in his turtleneck (342–43). Here are Joan's father, Paul, the Royal Porcupine, one version of her imaginary lover, and, finally, Arthur. Because they all collapse into one another, it is again made clear that a better man is not the solution to Joan/Felicia's need to be rescued. In fact, they all collapse into each because they are the projected rescuer figure of the helpless victim that Joan has found it so convenient to play: "But of course, all the characters in the romances are aspects of Joan, the male murderer as well" (Galloway 137). That the final transformation is into a skeleton makes it clear that her belief that meaning and safety only come from romantic relationships has been psychologically destroying Joan. Felicia, then, refuses to go through the door, and *Stalked by Love*'s plot comes to a standstill.

Joan, however, is no longer identified with Felicia. When the knock finally comes on her door, Joan considers her "options," starting with the most passive: "I could pretend I wasn't there. I could wait and do nothing. I could disguise my voice and say that I was someone else" (343). These have been her typical defences in the past. But, instead, she takes the offensive, opens the door, and hits the journalist on the head with a Cinzano bottle.

Atwood has always been firm about the social limits on the transformation of an individual. As she puts it in *Survival*, you can deny you are a victim of social constraints, or acknowledge these but see them as inevitable, or refuse to see these as inevitable, however powerful they may be, or be what she calls "a creative non-victim" (38). Several critics have assumed that the last position was, from her perspective, the best. And so it would be, except that, as she points out, "In an oppressed society, of course, you can't become an ex-victim — insofar as you are connected with your society — until the entire society's position has been changed" (*Survival* 38). To reach the last position before the society is liberated is only possible by "abandoning the society," something Atwood says is "a choice I do not find morally commendable" (*Second* 145). Thus, in Atwood's view, no one, however enlightened, who takes on a social role, can avoid social construction, victimization, or responsibility for victimizing others.

Critics are divided about whether Joan has achieved any insight by the end of the novel; certainly she has not achieved the position of a creative non-victim. But does she still see herself as the helpless victim of circumstances presented by her story? Clara Thomas points out that this story can only be the one told to the reporter, since at the end of the first paragraph of the novel, Joan remarks of her disappearing act, "At first I thought I'd managed it" (*Lady* 3; Thomas 161–62). She only discovers that she hasn't when she gets the mail on the last afternoon she spends in Terremoto. That evening, the journalist arrives. Thomas points out that the story still presents Joan as a fairly helpless victim:

> She said that she did not mean to go home with the Royal Porcupine, but she could not refuse to help him carry home a dead dog and so, once at his apartment, they made love. She hated and still hates her ensuing further deceit of Arthur, but she could not bear to give up the acted-out fantasies of her adventures with the Royal Porcupine. She says that she did not mean to tell the truth about her *Lady Oracle* poems to her interviewer, but she did tell him about their genesis in automatic writing and so created a sensation. (170)

She doesn't mean to do things, and the result, as Chuck Brewer points out, is that she's "like an out-of-control school bus." Typically, her reply is, "I don't mean to be" (272). Rather than consider what Chuck has said, as usual she slides out from accepting any responsibility. Part of seeing oneself as a helpless victim is denying that one can do anyone else any harm. But, of course, Joan's mother did Joan a good deal of harm, although she may well herself have been a victim first of poverty and unloving parents, then of an unwanted pregnancy, and finally of an unloving husband. And the "powerless" Joan leaves a trail of wounded men behind.

Critics are inclined to agree that Joan is still stuck in her victim role. Frank Davey notes that Joan "at the end of the book, as she impulsively rushes off to treat as a helpless young man the journalist she so recently perceived as a hired killer, . . . is about to throw away this discovery [that she projects good and evil personae on to others] and embark on a further illusion" (154). Lecker implies that she never gains any coherent sense of her own identity because she lives in a contemporary world that cannot sustain the myth of identity any longer: Atwood's novels are "about multi-faceted characters who are as fragmented and duplicitous as the times in which they live" (203). Godard feels that Joan finds herself when she accepts the multiplicity of her being (16, 21), but concludes that "she appears to be casting herself in a new role as nurse to the wounded journalist as plotted by Mavis Quilp" (34). Grace doubts that Joan has progressed at the end (117). Atwood herself says Joan develops "three quarters of an inch" ("Interview" [Struthers] 25). Joan appears to have once again fallen for her own romantic vision, this time a journalist in a bandage instead of an activist in a black turtleneck or an artist in a cloak.

However, she has told him more of the truth than she has ever told any other man, instead of pretending to have amnesia or running away while he was still unconscious, two possibilities she considers. Thus, she feels that he, unlike Arthur, is "the only person who knows anything about me." One thing he knows about her is her potential for violence: "I've never hit anyone else with a bottle, so they never got to see that part of me. Neither did I, come to think of it" (345). Although Atwood is clearly not advocating the wholesale beaning of intruding men with Cinzano bottles, this act clearly marks a breakthrough for Joan. Instead of retreating into the bathroom/womb, cowering in terror, she has fought back. She has refused to be a victim. But more than that, she has expressed her aggression and anger directly for the first time, and it hasn't led to total destruction. Up until now, her aggression has been expressed in her novels, just as little girls express their aggression mainly in words: "Words were not a prelude to war but the war itself, a devious, subterranean war that was unending because there were no decisive acts, no knock-down blows . . ." (53). Here, finally, Joan has expressed her fear of men by confronting danger instead of running away. In a sense, she has slain the Minotaur created by her projection of villany on to any man who fails to conform to her Gothic expectations. Despite his seven stitches, the man forgives her instead of pressing charges, and even after she has told her story, still seems inclined to be friendly. And she has taken responsibility for visiting him, as she plans to take responsibility for Sam and Marlene's predicament as well. And she seems capable of thinking about Arthur's reaction without the usual panic about rejection. What has changed?

Although Felicia retreats from the door, Joan goes through it, and to pass through this door is a metaphor for birth. As she waits, clutching her Cinzano bottle, she thinks: "It struck me that I'd spent too much of my life crouching behind closed doors, listening to the voices on the other side" (340). Instead of the passive role of the eavesdropper, of the floating foetus, she has finally moved out, however tentatively, into the world of adult responsibility. Her first step out of the door has led to a situation where she might have killed a man: responsibility indeed. But Joan does not flee. Even Atwood's comments indicate that Joan has made some kind of progress:

> Before she said I will hide who I am because nobody will like who I am. They will not accept me. . . . If I can conceal myself, then I will be safe. So she's gotten as far as saying I am who I am, take it or leave it, and the reason that she feels better with the fellow she's hit over the head with the bottle than with anybody else is that at least she knows, at least the new relationship will be on some kind of honest basis, if there is one. ("Interview" [Struthers] 25).

But although it is tempting to take this as the last word, one thing that contemporary criticism has established is that Atwood's inter-pretation of her own work can be no more valid than that of any other knowledgeable and insightful critic. After all, the kind of rationalization and self-delusion that Joan manifests does exist among real writers, too. Just as Joan can be mistaken about her motives and decisions, so can Atwood, or any writer. And what Atwood has put in her novel has left critics in serious disagreement. The majority, in fact, see Joan as having made no progress. That she hits the reporter with the bottle may not be evidence of a new self-assertion. Could it not simply be the mandatory scene where the threatened maiden defends her virtue by hitting the hero "with something (a candelabrum, a poker, a stone, any hard sharp object would do), knocking him out and inducing brain fever with hallucinations, during which his features and desires would be purified by suffering and he would murmur her name" (317–18)? If so, then the journalist has just stepped into Redmond/Arthur's place, and the plot rolls on. We are not given a definite answer, and the novel dissolves in a haze of tune-in-next-week questions: Will Joan and the journalist fall in love? Will she rescue Sam and Marlene? Perhaps we have just shifted into the world of soap opera from the world of romance, rather than having moved somewhat closer to complex, grey, shifting reality.

Between Reality and Fantasy

Robert Lecker notes that Joan's remark "I guess it will make a pretty weird story, once he's written it" (*Lady* 344) reveals that the whole novel is "ghost written" by the reporter (Lecker 194; see also Rule). If so, Joan's life, already heavily influenced by literary patterns, transmitted by a character who cheerfully admits she didn't tell "very many" lies to the reporter (whose profession has already been satirized for over-dramatization) (344), can only be connected to reality by the thinnest of threads (see Lecker 194). According to Lecker, the point this complex narrative is intended to convey is that "reality and fantasy are one, and to believe that it is possible to escape from either is the greatest delusion" (198). In fact, to believe that there can be a conclusive interpretation is a form of the Gothic thinking that Atwood wrote the novel to combat (cf. McMillan 63). Critics eager to decide one way or another are simply falling into her trap, revealing once again the human desire for clear answers. But Atwood is like Aunt Lou: "the bits of wisdom she dispensed could have several meanings, when you thought hard about them" (86).

In fact, as Lecker, Godard, Givner and Hite imply, Atwood is trying to disrupt our belief in a whole set of dualisms, including the reality/fantasy duality. Godard puts it this way: "Joan, in *Lady Oracle*, plays with triple mirrors, which disrupt any temptation to dualism, opening up an infinity of perspectives that eventually encompass all the characters of the novel..." (17). But to move from the idea that there are clear-cut dualisms, to the idea that dualisms fragment into multiplicity, or that "reality and fantasy are one" (Lecker 198), is to run the risk of setting up another dualism. Before we had reality (good) and fantasy (bad); now we have dualism (bad, or at least outdated and impossible) and multiplicity or unity (good, or at least inevitable). What Atwood substitutes for these dualisms, however, and this is what makes her so tricky to read, is duplicity. As Eli Mandel puts it: "Duplicity, in part, consists in trying to have it both ways" (142). At first, this just sounds like Joan, trying to have her cake and eat it too. But it means that issues are complicated, that each answer can only be worked out in its particular context, that there are no rules that will guarantee innocence, and thus we will always make mistakes and then have to accept responsibility for them. Or, in Joan's words, "It did make a mess; but then, I don't think I'll ever be a very tidy person" (345). Atwood undermines the idea that there is only one reality and the idea that there is only one self. She also shows us that some versions of reality are more powerful than others. For example, we realize that Joan's versions of self were most often constructed either by men or, through her mother and her education, for men. As for reality, she admits "I'd always found other people's versions of reality very influential" (161).

Many critics simply assume, as does Catherine Stimpson, that Atwood "says that we must recognize reality and distinguish it clearly from falsehoods, fiction, and fantasy" (40). If this is what Atwood is saying, she certainly has picked an odd way to say it. In the last pages of the novel, on reading the lawyer's letter, Joan concludes that "I should have stayed where I was and faced reality" (339). But clearly reality won't be that easy to face, since Mr. Morgan, the eyewitness to Joan's false suicide, "acting out his own fantasy," concludes that Sam and Marlene had pushed Joan off the boat (338). And at the time, of course, Sam and Marlene believed they were saving Joan from being arrested for taking part in their plot to bomb the Peace Bridge, and Joan that she is escaping from an unknown sexual harrasser. If Joan returns to Toronto to face a court, she will again face a powerful version of reality forged by powerful men. The final decision about which fantasy is closest to the truth will be made in a legal context, with pages of testimony, where many fantasies will be compared in order to pick the one that seems closest to the current legal version of reality. But even in this context, where the most painstaking procedures are followed to ensure that something close to the truth emerges, the innocent are sometimes found guilty and the guilty innocent. Indeed, given her scattered and self-deprecating narrative style, Joan may find her story downplayed because it lacks the single-minded conviction of someone who believes that there is only one version of the truth.

Nonetheless, a court of law must hand down a decision. Someone must take responsibility. In literary criticism and theory it is possible to see ambiguity, multiplicity, and open-endedness as virtues, as creative and liberating. Joan realizes that it is impossible to try to distinguish the authentic from the mask long before the end of the novel: "I . . . decided that . . . hidden depths should remain hidden; façades were at least as truthful" (197). To see the world as multiple, or as a mix of fantasy and reality, is probably less mistaken than believing that there is only one correct view of it. But when we move into the ordinary world where we must decide what to do and how to behave, then the insight that the world is multiple, or an indeterminate mix, can become overwhelming. It is easy to use this perspective as a way of arguing that any behaviour can be justified, another form of escape. Social reality does, for example, curb Joan's desire to succeed as a fat ballet dancer, and sometimes that social reality, however crazy and unfair it seems, will have to temper our vision of multiplicity, and may actively interfere with our desires. Justice and morality depend on our learning to think hard about our choices, and about the social constructions of reality rather than resorting to some version of Gothic thinking, or worse, pretending we can avoid making choices or that our choices make no difference.

Joan's realization that she has to live in a socially constructed fantasy world rather than in her own solitary one may well be the legacy of Aunt Lou. At the reading of the will, Joan wonders whether Aunt Lou had disapproved of Joan's fatness all along; however, Aunt Lou may just realize how severe a handicap fat can be to a woman. Joan's desire to be a fat ballerina may be all very well at the level of individual fantasy, but ill judged at the level of social reality. It is ultimately difficult to decide, because Aunt Lou's advice resembles the enigmatic messages transmitted by the sybils from the gods. (It was a sybil who gave Aeneas the golden bough that allowed him safe passage to the underworld.) The messages of the gods (and remember Joan's affection for Mercury, another one of the gods' messengers) are invariably tricky to decipher. In fact, one school of biblical, legal, and literary interpretation has been called *hermeneutics*, a term that incorporates one of Mercury's alternate names, Hermes, and means "messages from the gods."

Good interpretation, even the kind that promotes multiplicity and the awareness of the interconnectedness of socially-constructed reality and individual fantasy, still involves an examination of the text, a careful argument leading to a conclusion, and a consideration of the opinions of others. In the context of ordinary life, decisions also must be made on the basis of careful interpretations, and responsibility must be taken, however certain it is that our imperfect knowledge will lead to mistakes.

The Royal Porcupine and Joan: Gothic Thinkers

In many ways, the Royal Porcupine seems the most attractive man in the novel. When Joan and the Porcupine meet, they are at similar stages of their careers, they are similarly notorious, and they even look alike, both redheaded and dramatically dressed, she in a long, red dress and he in evening attire with black cape and spats. They seem the perfect couple. However, Joan herself sees them as an impossible match, even before Chuck kills his Royal Porcupine identity, commenting

> It wasn't that I didn't love him. I did, in a peculiar way, but I knew I couldn't live with him. For him, reality and fantasy were the same thing, which meant that for him there was no reality. But for me it would mean that there was no fantasy, and therefore no escape. (272)

Interestingly, she is using the Royal Porcupine in much the same way as Paul used her: as an escape.

The novel seems to support the split that Joan hypothesizes between reality and fantasy, giving us Arthur, the dull, grey reality, and the Royal Porcupine, the colourful fantasy. However, can we trust Joan's view of the world? Clearly not. This is the Joan who believes in many other simplistic and destructive ideas: a woman can't be a successful artist and a happy wife, men are either heroes or villains, and so forth. But the point is, she is not alone in her beliefs, and in the world of human relationships such beliefs can have terrible consequences. (Think about the fantasy lives of mass murderers for a moment.)

Joan puts forward several models to try to maintain her belief in duality. The simplest is that some people are all good and others are all bad. Then there are those who switch back and forth, such as her father, who killed during the war, and now saves lives, but who also switches from a powerful doctor at work to an "inconsequential fool" at home (138). Arthur moves in a manic-depressive way from one political philosophy to the next: "Arthur was a sequence" (213). Joan shuttles frantically between Arthur and the Royal Porcupine:

When I was with Arthur, the Royal Porcupine seemed like a daydream from one of my less credible romances, with an absurdity about him that I tried to exclude from my fictions. But when I was with the Royal Porcupine, he seemed plausible and solid. Everything he did and said made sense in his own terms, whereas it was Arthur who became unreal; he faded to an insubstantial ghost, a washed-out photo on some mantelpiece I'd long ago abandoned. Was I hurting him, was I being unfaithful? How could you hurt a photograph? (261)

Joan's inability to see either of them as "gray and multidimensional and complicated like everyone else" is a function of their involvement with her (271). If they were complicated, she would have to pay attention to them, to interpret them in order to understand how they differ from her stereotyped view. (One of the attractive things for her about both Paul and the Royal Porcupine is that they cooperate in producing themselves as simple characters; they, like her, actively play roles.) Just as acting as an adult threatens her with the unpleasant problems of responsibility and guilt, so treating others as real means the same thing. Actors, like photographs, do not really suffer, bleed, or die. The curtain falls and they wipe off their makeup, hang up their costumes, and go home to domestic reality. People, however, live their roles.

When Chuck Brewer kills the Royal Porcupine, cutting his hair and shaving his beard, he is preceding Joan to limbo, where she cuts her hair and dyes it "mud brown" (314). Chuck has turned himself into a victim by pretending he thinks his Brewer persona is what Joan wants (although he knows better, having said "If I was reasonable, you wouldn't love me" [266]). He turns her into a thing and accuses her of being a threat (269, 270), employing the same tactics she herself used on her mother. Both Joan and Chuck are making some progress when they commit their symbolic suicides, in that they acknowledge that their habitual patterns of behaviour don't get them the love they want. But this is just a beginning, and we do not see how either of them resolves the problem. Neither of them can believe that fantasy constructs and interacts with social reality: instead they commit a kind of symbolic amputation, a form of suicide, rather than attempt to integrate the two.

"Reality," the "real self," and so forth, are easy to say, but difficult to describe, because, as the novel makes clear, much of reality exists in the human mind's perception of it, a mind full of advertisements, fairy tales, memories, desires — all inevitably undermining the idea that anyone has access to pure reality. Although some versions and some parts of reality seem more plausible than others, or more widespread, none exists outside some form of human society. Joan's problem is not in facing reality, but in working out some of the connections between two concepts that she has tried to keep completely separate. She needs a version of reality that is less self-destructive and less socially irresponsible. But Atwood is not proposing a more conformist position. If we choose as our version of reality the average, what everybody thinks, we will end up subject to what Rowland Smith calls "mediocrity triumphant, the average rampant" (142), a world covered in plastic, the dead world of a museum or a store window. We will, like Chuck Brewer, have destroyed all that's interesting and colourful about ourselves: our creativity, our art, our culture. Fantasy and reality need to be played off against each other, not further divided.

Why do Joan and the Royal Porcupine go to such extremes to maintain an ultimately impossible distinction? Both of them have used fantasy, the Royal Porcupine more publicly than Joan, to avoid responsibility. She avoids the serious emotional commitment that the shallow relationships of popular romance glide over in their happily-ever-after endings, and takes minimal responsibility for her serious writing or her publication (even trying to back out of her contract at the last minute). He avoids any serious romantic commitment in choosing only married women for his affairs, and makes no political commitment: "he thought politics were boring, especially Canadian nationalism: 'Art is universal,' he'd say. 'They're just trying to get attention' " (262). (As if *he* wasn't.) So Arthur spits on a policeman, the Royal Porcupine puts dead animals on display in freezers and blows up the dynamite, and Joan, in a more private realm, first overeats and then burns the dinners. That the result is the kind of self-defeating and negative attention offered to naughty or deliberately inept children doesn't bother them, because none of them is ready to cope with for the serious attention paid to purposeful acts, acts for which one must take responsibility. Atwood's comment on this behaviour, I venture to say, is summed up in the remark of the union organizer: "I know you kids mean well, but believe me. Sometimes the wrong kind of help is worse than no help at all" (262).

Mirror and Frame Confusion

In the introduction to her tangled tale, Joan compares her life to "the frame of a baroque mirror" (3). This sort of introduction in fiction is actually called a "frame" because it indicates to us who is telling, or framing, the story, and, in this case, at the end, why. But art, as Aristotle said, supposedly imitates life, or as Shakespeare's Hamlet put it "hold[s] . . . the mirror up to nature" (3.2.23). Thus, in her account, Joan holds the mirror up to her life, which is compared to the frame of a mirror. The account is the story of how a desire for neatness and control led, instead, to incredible confusion. The task, apparently simple for Aristotle, of reflecting nature in art, lurches out of control in a set of metaphors that make it clear that frames don't work, that life, and even the language that is supposed to tame it, bulge out past the constraint constructed for them by our desire for order and clear answers. The frame that is supposed to mark the division between reality and art, and the simple division between reality and fantasy that the mirror metaphor appears to make possible, have both been completely taken apart. Atwood is trying to break it to us that we are all "closed out from that impossible white paradise where love was as final as death, and banished to this other place where everything change[s] and shift[s]" (286). Faced with multiplicity, with a reality constructed through fantasy, we will have to struggle over and over again to read better, to think more clearly, and to love more honestly, all in the knowledge that we will not only make mistakes, but also that we will have to take responsibility for them.

Works Cited

Amiel, Barbara. "Once More the Poor WASP Heroine." Rev. of *Lady Oracle*. *Maclean's* 6 Sept. 1976: 68.
   A negative review, suggesting that WASPs (white Anglo-Saxon Protestants) are too dull to provide interesting characters for novels.

Aspinall, Dawn. "Homage to the Colonial Mentality." *This Magazine* Aug. 1973: 16–17.

Atwood, Margaret. *Cat's Eye*. Toronto: McClelland, 1988. Novel.

_____ . *The Edible Woman*. New Canadian Library 93 1969. Toronto: McClelland, 1973. Novel.

_____ . "Great Unexpectations: An Autobiographical Foreword." Van-Spanckeren and Castro xiii–xvi.

_____ . "An Interview with Margaret Atwood." With J.R. (Tim) Struthers. *Essays on Canadian Writing* 6 (1977): 18–27. An excellent interview.

_____ . "*Lady Oracle*." Box 23, ts. Margaret Atwood Papers. Thomas Fisher Rare Book Library, U of Toronto. An early draft of the novel.

_____ . "Interview with Margaret Atwood." With Linda Sandler. *Margaret Atwood: A Symposium*. Ed. Sandler. Spec. issue of *Malahat Review* 41 (1977): 7–27. A helpful interview with good insights into *Lady Oracle*.

_____ . *Lady Oracle*. 1976. Toronto: Seal-McClelland-Bantam, 1977. Novel.

_____ . "Margaret Atwood." *Canadian Writers at Work: Interviews with Geoff Hancock*. Toronto: Oxford UP, 1987. 256–87. An interesting interview, with a brief look at *Lady Oracle*.

_____ . "Margaret Atwood." With Graeme Gibson. *Eleven Canadian Novelists*. Toronto: Anansi, 1973. 1–31. Useful comments on the Gothic.

_____ . *Margaret Atwood: Conversations*. Ed. Earl G. Ingersoll. Ontario Review Press Critical Series. Willowdale, ON: Firefly, 1990. Long selection from a wide range of important interviews including Gibson, Hancock, Sandler, and Struthers. A useful source for interviews published in hard-to-find publications.

_____ . " 'My Craft and Sullen Art': The Writers Speak. Margaret Atwood." *Atlantis: A Women's Studies Journal* 4.1 (1978): 161–63.

_____ . "A Reply." *Signs: Journal of Women in Culture and Society* 2.2 (1976): 340–41.

_____. "Royal Porcupine's Identikit." (Letter to the editor.) *Saturday Night* Jan.–Feb. 1977: 3.

_____. *Second Words: Selected Critical Prose.* Toronto: Anansi, 1982. Criticism.

_____. *Surfacing.* Toronto: McClelland, 1972. Novel.

_____. *Survival: A Thematic Guide to Canadian Liteature.* Toronto: Anansi, 1972. Criticism.

Austen, Jane. *Northanger Abbey.* Ed. Anne Henry Ehrenpreis. Harmondsworth, Eng.: Penguin, 1978.

Belkin, Roslyn. "The Worth of the Shadow: Margaret Atwood's *Lady Oracle*." *Thalia* 1.3 (1979): 3–8.

Explicates the humour in *Lady Oracle* through the writings of Luigi Pirandello.

Beran, Carol L. "George, Leda, and a Poured Concrete Balcony: A Study of Three Aspects of the Evolution of *Lady Oracle*." *Canadian Literature* 112 (1987): 18–28.

A study of the manuscripts of *Lady Oracle* that discusses the effect of changing the narration from an account directed at Arthur to one directed at the reader, the addition of the character of Leda Sprott, and the revision of the first paragraph.

Berger, Peter L., and Thomas Luckmann. *The Social Construction of Reality: A Treatise in the Sociology of Knowledge.* 1966. Harmondsworth, Eng.: Pelican, 1984.

Berne, Eric. *Games People Play: The Psychology of Human Relationships.* New York: Grove, 1964.

Bromberg, Pamela S. "The Two Faces of the Mirror in *The Edible Woman* and *Lady Oracle*." VanSpanckeren and Castro 12–23.

Feminist study of mirrors and the male gaze.

Brophy, Brigid. "A Contrary Critic Takes a Crack at *Lady Oracle*." Rev. of *Lady Oracle. Globe and Mail* 9 Oct. 1976: 33.

A negative review that nonetheless notes features of the novel that deserve careful consideration.

Carrington, Ildikó de Papp. "Margaret Atwood." *Canadian Writers and Their Works.* Ed. Robert Lecker, Jack David, and Ellen Quigley. Fiction Series vol. 9. Downsview, ON.: ECW, 1987. 25–116. 10 vols. to date. 1983– .

A clear account of the novel's structure and of its relations to Atwood's earlier work. Focuses on the theme of costumes, dancing, and writing. A detailed examination of the maze symbol relates Joan's goddess figure to Rider Haggard's novel *She.*

Cluett, Robert. "Surface Structures: The Syntactic Profile of *Surfacing*." *Margaret Atwood: Language, Text, and System.* Ed. Sherrill E. Grace and Lorraine Weir. Vancouver: U of British Columbia P, 1983. 67–90.

An analysis of Atwood's sentence structure in *Surfacing* that concludes that the style is extraordinarily plain, even for Atwood.

Coleridge, Samuel Taylor. "Dejection: An Ode." *The Norton Anthology of English Literature*. Ed. M.H. Abrams, et al. 4th ed. Vol. 2. New York: Norton, 1979. 373–77. 2 vols.

Cude, Wilfrid. "Bravo Mothball!: An Essay on *Lady Oracle*." *The Canadian Novel: Here and Now*. Ed. John Moss. Toronto: NC, 1978. 45–50.

>Praises Atwood for making it clear that Joan is to be seen as an essentially negative character.

_____ "Nobody Dunit: The Loose End as Structural Element in *Lady Oracle*." *Journal of Canadian Studies* 15.1 (1980): 30–44.

>Cude, by casting Joan's behaviour in the most negative light possible, reveals the damage done by "innocent" victims.

Davey, Frank. "*Lady Oracle*'s Secret: Atwood's Comic Novels." *Surviving the Paraphrase: Eleven Essays on Canadian Literature*. Winnipeg: Turnstone, 1983. 151–66.

>Deals with *The Edible Woman*, *Surfacing*, and *Lady Oracle*, relating all of them to comedy because their endings, although not the typical reconciliation of lovers and families found at the end of most comedies, portray a heroine better prepared to deal with society and, however marginally, more aware of her own failings.

Davidson, Arnold E., and Cathy N. Davidson. *The Art of Margaret Atwood: Essays in Criticism*. Toronto: Anansi, 1981.

>Useful collection, including Lecker and Thomas on *Lady Oracle*.

_____ . "Margaret Atwood's *Lady Oracle*: The Artist as Escapist and Seer." *Studies in Canadian Literature* 3 (1978): 166–77.

>A good early account that makes many points that subsequent writers find it necessary to repeat.

Engel, Marian. "She Who Laughs Last . . . ." Rev. of *Lady Oracle*. *Tamarack Review* 69 (1976): 94–96.

>A positive review, defending the novel as witty social satire.

Freibert, Lucy M. "The Artist as Picaro: The Revelation of Margaret Atwood's *Lady Oracle*." *Canadian Literature* 92 (1982): 23–33.

>A useful article that sets the novel in the picaresque tradition, focusing on Joan's activity, rather than on her passivity.

Fulford, Robert. "Derring Do." *Saturday Night* Nov. 1976: 46.

>An account of the novel's roman à clef features. See also page 38 in this issue for a brief allusion to the work.

Galloway, Priscilla. Rev. of *Lady Oracle*. *Canadian Book Review Annual 1976*. Ed. Dean Tudor et al. Toronto: PMA, 1977. 136–37.

>A positive review that notes the serial publication in *Redbook* (Aug. 1976) of an abridged version of the novel.

Givner, Jessie. "Mirror Images in Margaret Atwood's *Lady Oracle*." *Studies in Canadian Literature* 14.1 (1989): 139–46.

Connects mirror images both to French feminist criticism and to the novel's refusal of closure.

Godard, Barbara. "My (m)Other, My Self: Strategies for Subversion in Atwood and Hébert." *Essays on Canadian Writing* 26 (1983): 13–44.

Concentrates on the importance of the mother-daughter relationship, while connecting the novel not only to Anne Hébert's *Kamouraska*, but also to a wide range of feminist writing.

Grace, Sherrill E. "More Than a Very Double Life." *Violent Duality: A Study of Margaret Atwood*. Montreal: Véhicule, 1980. 111–28.

Grace gives some details on the novel's composition, and then works through an interpretation that adds details on the maze and on the relation of the novel to the Bluebeard story.

Greenwood, Michael. "Mark Prent." *Artscanada* 166 – 167 – 168 (1972): 39–41.

Hite, Molly. Ch. 4. "Other Side, Other Woman: Lady Oracle." *The Other Side of the Story: Structures and Strategies of Contemporary Feminist Narrative*. Ithaca: Cornell UP, 1989. 127–67.

Hite considers why contemporary women writers like Jean Rhys, Alice Walker, and Doris Lessing do not normally write postmodernist texts, stating that the implications of their innovations in narrative form are even more radical than the postmodernist ones undertaken mainly by male authors. In her discussion of *Lady Oracle* she states that the novel's refusal to provide a straightforward resolution to the plot or an explanation of various "appearances" of the Goddess in the form of Joan's mother or the Fat Lady aligns it with French feminist discussions of "feminine excess."

Hoeppner, Kenneth. "Frye's Theory of Romance, Popular Romance, and Atwood's *Lady Oracle*." *Contemporary Commonwealth Fiction* (ACLALS bulletin) 8th ser. 1 (1989): 74–87.

Compares Janice Radway's ideas about popular romance with Northrop Frye's about romance, to conclude that the two may achieve similar ends.

Irby, James E. Introduction. *Labyrinths: Selected Stories and Other Writings*. By Jorge Luis Borges. Ed. Donald A. Yates and Irby. New Directions Paperbook 186. New York: New Directions, 1964. xv–xxiii.

Jensen, Emily. "Margaret Atwood's *Lady Oracle*: A Modern Parable." *Essays on Canadian Writing* 33 (1986): 29–49.

The best treatment of the allusions to "The Red Shoes" (movie and fairy tale), "The Little Mermaid," and "The Lady of Shalott," as well as the Fat Lady fantasies and the multiple endings of the Felicia-Charlotte struggle. Jensen also deals with Joan's need for male approval for her writing (which is represented in the Fat Lady fantasies as dancing, tightrope walking, and skating).

Johnston, Sue Ann. "The Daughter as Escape Artist." *Atlantis: A Women's Studies Journal* 9.2 (1984): 10–22.

An examination of the mother-daughter relationship.

Keith, W.J. "Margaret Atwood." *A Sense of Style: Studies in the Art of Fiction in English-Speaking Canada*. Toronto: ECW, 1989. 175–94.

Keith's chapter on Atwood points out the traditional qualities of her concerns, and examines in detail the parodic qualities of *Lady Oracle*. Keith includes especially helpful insights into allusions to other Canadian works.

Langer, Beryl Donaldson. "Class and Gender in Margaret Atwood's Fiction." *Australian-Canadian Studies* 6 (1988): 73–101.

A discussion of the "new class" that has grown up between labour and capital. Although salaried, like workers, members of this class have "cultural capital" and serve the function of reproducing capitalist cultural relations and class differences. The contradictory position of this class is seen as accounting for Atwood's irony and the fragmented and alienated lives of her characters.

Lecker, Robert. "Janus through the Looking Glass: Atwood's First Three Novels." Davidson and Davidson, *Art* 177–203.

An excellent corrective to those articles that state or imply that all Joan needs to do is stop confusing fantasy and reality, and settle down to being a wholesome, integrated self.

MacDonald, Larry. "Psychologism and the Philosophy of Progress: The Recent Fiction of MacLennan, Davies and Atwood." *Studies in Canadian Literature* 9.2 (1984): 121–43.

Atwood clearly depicts many of the problems that come from the liberal belief in the preeminence of individual freedom and the inevitable success of technology (one wreaks havoc on minorities, the other on nature). MacDonald feels, however, that Atwood simplistically attempts to find the solution to these problems in individual psychological breakthrough.

Maclean, Susan. "*Lady Oracle*: The Art of Reality and the Reality of Art." *Journal of Canadian Fiction* 28–29 (1980): 179–97.

Interesting, but diffuse.

McCombs, Judith. "Atwood's Fictive Portraits: From Victim to Surfacer, From Oracle to Birth." *Women's Studies* 12 (1986): 69–88.

Discusses Atwood's work so far in the context of the formation of the artist.

McMillan, Ann. "The Transforming Eye: *Lady Oracle* and Gothic Tradition." VanSpanckeren and Castro 48–64.

An account of the tradition of the Gothic and of its subsequent feminist interpretation, which leads to insights helpfully applied to *Lady Oracle*.

Mandel, Eli. "Atwood Gothic." *Margaret Atwood: A Symposium*. Ed. Linda Sandler. Spec. issue of *Malahat Review* 41 (1977): 165–74

Although Mandel does not mention *Lady Oracle*, this essay situates Atwood's use of Gothic in a wider tradition.

Miller, Jane. "A Pack of Truths." Rev. of *Lady Oracle*. *Times Literary Supplement* 15 July 1977: 872.

Sees some of the novel's cleverness undermined by our difficulty in seeing Joan as a liar.

Miner, Valerie. "Atwood in Metamorphosis: An Authentic Canadian Fairy Tale." *Her Own Woman: Profiles of Ten Canadian Women.* Ed. Myrna Kostash. Toronto: Macmillan, 1975. 173–94.

Interesting information contained in a rather gushing account.

Modleski, Tania. *Loving with a Vengeance: Mass-Produced Fantasies for Women.* New York: Methuen, 1982.

Morley, Patricia. "The Gothic as Social Realism." Rev. of *Lady Oracle. Canadian Forum* Dec.–Jan. 1976–77: 49–50.

A positive review: "Atwood's novel is a statement of the necessity, for men and women alike, of inner freedom, self-reliance, and growth" (50).

Northey, Margot. *The Haunted Wilderness: The Gothic and Grotesque in Canadian Fiction.* Toronto: U of Toronto P, 1976.

Does not mention *Lady Oracle,* but helpful on the Canadian Gothic.

Owen, I.M. "Queen of the Maze." Rev. of *Lady Oracle. Books in Canada* Sept. 1976: 3–5.

A long, positive review that comments, however, that the characters' positive emotions are undercut because they "can't tell about the feeling without a self-deprecating sneer" (5).

Patton, Marilyn. "*Lady Oracle*: The Politics of the Body." *ARIEL* 22.4 (1991): 29–48.

Focuses on Atwood's conception of the writer, the muse, and the Goddess.

Pollitt, Katha. Rev. of *Lady Oracle. New York Times Book Review* 26 Sept. 1976: 7–8. A negative review. *Lady Oracle* offers "the stock figures and pat insights of a certain kind of popular feminist-oriented fiction."

Radway, Janice A. *Reading the Romance: Women, Patriarchy and Popular Literature.* Chapel Hill: U of North Carolina P, 1984.

Rigney, Barbara Hill. "The 'Escape Artist': *Lady Oracle.*" *Margaret Atwood.* London: Macmillan Education, 1987. 62–81.

Argues that Joan avoids facing reality by indulging in escapist art. Interesting examination of the themes of red shoes and dancing girls with respect to this and other works. Deals with the "Lady of Shalott" allusions.

Rosenberg, Jerome H. *Margaret Atwood.* Twayne's World Authors Series 740. Boston: Twayne, 1984.

A brief overview of the novel.

Rosengarten, Herbert. "Urbane Comedy." Rev. of *Lady Oracle. Canadian Literature* 72 (1977): 84–87.

A positive review.

Rosowski, Susan J. "Margaret Atwood's *Lady Oracle*: Fantasy and the Modern Gothic Novel." Critical Essays on World Literature. *Critical Essays on Margaret Atwood.* Ed. Judith McCombs. Boston: G.K. Hall, 1988. 197–208.

An examination of the Gothic elements of the novel.

Ross, Catherine Sheldrick. "'Banished to this Other Place': Atwood's *Lady Oracle.*" *English Studies in Canada* 6 (1980): 460–74.

Focuses on the art-reality split, with some interesting comments on the novel's allusions to *Alice through the Looking Glass*, by Lewis Carroll.

———. "Calling Back the Ghost of the Old-Time Heroine: Duncan, Montgomery, Atwood, Laurence and Munro." *Studies in Canadian Literature* 4.1 (1979): 43–58.

Draws some interesting connections between Joan and another redheaded romance reader and writer, Anne of Green Gables.

Rubenstein, Roberta. "Escape Artists and Split Personalities: Margaret Atwood." *Boundaries of the Self: Gender, Culture, Fiction*. Urbana: U of Illinois P, 1987. 63–122.

A detailed and helpful comparative feminist account of all Atwood's novels (excluding *Cat's Eye*) focusing on the problems Atwood's characters have in dealing with identity, doubling, splitting, engulfment, and so forth.

Rule, Jane. "Life, Liberty and the Pursuit of Normalcy: The Novels of Margaret Atwood." *Margaret Atwood: A Symposium*. Ed. Linda Sandler. Spec. issue of *Malahat Review* 41 (1977): 42–49

The first to suggest that "we must regard Joan's revelations, not as the final truth about the narrator, but as raw material for yet another story about her, to be told this time by the young reporter — another version of the lie that language is . . ." (49).

Sciff-Zamara, Roberta. "The Re/Membering of the Female Power in *Lady Oracle*." *Canadian Literature* 112 (1987): 32–38.

Connects the novel to the myth of the Goddess.

Slopen, Beverley. "Margaret Atwood." *Publisher's Weekly* 23 Aug. 1976: 6–8.

Part review, part account of a visit to Atwood shortly after the publication of *Lady Oracle*, heralds Atwood as the "superstar of Canadian letters."

Smith, Rowland. "Margaret Atwood: The Stoic Comedian." *Margaret Atwood: A Symposium*. Ed. Linda Sandler. Spec. issue of *Malahat* 41 (1977) 134–44.

Sees the novel as tragic: "the wry, stoic mask of the inept, attractive, alluring, dangling narrator in *Lady Oracle* covers a prolonged scream of pain" (144).

Solecki, Sam. "Letters in Canada 1976: Fiction." *University of Toronto Quarterly* 46 (1977): 343–44.

A negative review. The novel, "a slight comic" one, has been overpraised, the characters are uninteresting, the plot stale. Solecki notes, like MacDonald, that Atwood satirizes characters "whose political orientation — her orientation — is nationalistic without offering the reader a positive political or ideological alternative" (344). However, Solecki comments that the novel is structurally successful.

Spector, Judith A. "The Fatal Lady in Margaret Atwood's *Lady Oracle*." *University of Hartford Studies in Literature* 17.3 (1985): 33–44.

Sees both Joan and her mother as versions of the *femme fatale* like Keats's "belle dame sans merci." However, this fatal woman is often destructive to herself, as is Sylvia Plath's Lady Lazarus.

Stewart, Grace. *A New Mythos: The Novel of the Artist as Heroine, 1877–1977.* Monographs in Women's Studies. Montreal: Eden, 1979

Although a good deal of the material on the novel is summary, Stewart does set Joan into the context of other novels about women writers trying to escape male stereotypes.

Stimpson, Catharine R. "Don't Bother Me, I'm Dead." Rev. of *Lady Oracle. Ms.* Oct. 1976: 36, 40.

A superficial review.

Thomas, Clara. "*Lady Oracle*: The Narrative of a Fool-Heroine." Davidson and Davidson, *Art* 159–75.

Coins the label "Fool-Heroine" by analogy with Ellen Moers's labels in *Literary Women* (1976). A helpful general account, which connects well with Freibert. Discusses Joan's unreliability as a narrator, and works through the narrative itself in a helpful way.

VanSpanckeren, Kathryn, and Jan Garden Castro, eds. *Margaret Atwood: Vision and Forms.* Carbondale: Southern Illinois UP, 1988.

A useful collection; see Bromberg and McMillan.

Vincent, Sybil Korff. "The Mirror and the Cameo: Margaret Atwood's Comic/ Gothic Novel, *Lady Oracle.*" *The Female Gothic.* Ed. Juliann E. Fleenor. Montreal: Eden, 1983. 153–63.

Discusses how the humour of the novel deflates its Gothic menace. Interesting discussion of the imagery of clothing and objects in the Gothic tradition.

Wilson, Sharon R. "The Fragmented Self in *Lady Oracle.*" *Commonwealth Novel in English* 1 (1982): 50–85.

Uses psychoanalytic theories of narcissism to illuminate the novel.

York, Lorraine M. "Lives of Joan and Del: Separate Paths to Transformation in *Lives of Girls and Women* and *Lady Oracle.*" *University of Windsor Review* 19.2 (1986): 1–10.

A comparison of the ways in which Joan and Del, of Alice Munro's *Lives of Girls and Women*, transcend the image of the Tennysonian heroines: Princess Ida, Mariana of the moated grange, and the Lady of Shalott.

Updated checklists of Atwood scholarship are now published annually in the *Newsletter of the Margaret Atwood Society*, edited by Jerome Rosenberg, Department of English, Miami University, Akron, Ohio.

Index

94

MARGARET ATWOOD'S LADY ORACLE

Canadian Fiction Studies

Other volumes are in preparation